THINKING TOOLS

Second Edition

Academic, Personal, and Career Applications

Curtis Miles
Jane Rauton
Piedmont Technical College
Greenwood, South Carolina

H&H Publishing Company, Inc.
Clearwater, Florida

Cover Art:
Smithsonian Institute
Painting by Crockett Johnson

Editing, Production, and Interior Design:
Katherine Savige

Editorial Assistant:
Sally Marston

Promotion and Cover Design:
Thomas M. Howland

Production and Sales Management:
Robert D. Hackworth, Joseph W. Howland

Business Management:
Janie D. Howland

Printing and Binding:
R.R. Donnelley & Sons Co.

Library of Congress Cataloging-in-Publication Data

Miles, Curtis.
Thinking tools.

1. Thought and thinking. I. Rauton, Jane.
II. Title.
B105.T54M54 1987 160 87-219
ISBN 0-943202-23-X

Printing is the lowest number: 10 9 8 7 6 5 4 3 2 1

Contents

Chapter 4

Cause-And-Effect Thinking 92

Chapter 5

Testing Possibilities 126

Chapter 6

Thinking About Relevance 162

Chapter 7

Chapter 8

Chapter 9

Classification Charts 300

Chapter 10

Thinking With Sequences 330

Chapter 11

Thinking: The Ability And The Will 360

Preface

Our minds work continuously no matter what we do. Our choice is never whether or not to think. Our choice is to think well or to think poorly.

All of us know the basics of thinking; we have done it since infancy. We do not need to be taught thinking skills as a new enterprise. Rather, our need is to become conscious of our thinking skills, to practice and expand them, and to gain confidence in ourselves as effective thinkers in academic, personal, and career situations.

The title suggests the focus of this book. All of us have an array of multipurpose Thinking Tools which we use when tackling a choice, problem, business decision, or academic assignment. All of us use these tools naturally and constantly — we cannot help it. Those who think well have usually become conscious of some of the tools in their mental toolkits. Those who think poorly have usually never looked.

Thinking Tools arose from a gradual realization that most other textbooks related to thinking fall into three traps. Many talk about thinking; this is no more useful than reading about a sport without playing it. Many teach thinking skills as a contrived academic subject, easy to memorize and easy to forget. Many present snapshots of facts and activities and then move on to the next topic, without giving sufficient opportunity to discover, exercise, and master particular skills. Thinking Tools tries to avoid these traps, with your help.

The book is an invitation to look at many dimensions of your thinking toolkit. Over 80 exercises, covering eight specific skills and several dozen broad thinking tools, invite you to master your own thinking processes in the only way you can; by thinking and then reflecting on what your mind has done. In this process you will discover many of your mental techniques, give them names, practice and amplify them, and learn when and how to use them in academic, personal, and job situations. As with many worthwhile things, you will get out of Thinking Tools just about as much as you put into it.

We did not birth this book alone; many assisted and prodded along the way. We would like to express our thanks to our colleagues at Piedmont Technical College, to our families, and to the reviewers: Jerry Coleman, Union College, New Jersey; Howard Green Community College of the Finger Lakes, New York; Edward Wightman, Hudson Valley Community college, New York; Jo Ann Gardener, York Technical College, South Carolina; and Anna Berg, Passaic County Community College, New Jersey.

Thanks are also due the editors, and to many throughout a national network who have suggested the paths which this book follows. Two among very many deserve special mention: Claire Weinstein, who gave us a great conceptual boost, and Doree Pitkin, who as editor went vastly beyond the call of duty.

Curtis Miles
Jane Rauton

Greenwood, South Carolina
August, 1987

Chapter One

Introduction To Basic Thinking Skills

Our minds are constantly active. Our first need is to become aware of and observe this activity.

Think about these situations:

- buying a car.
- choosing a career.
- going for a job interview.
- studying for an exam.
- maintaining a relationship with someone who is angry with you.

Most of us are familiar with these circumstances. When we face them we need to think carefully. We may not notice we are thinking about them, but we are. Our minds instinctively become active when confronted with a decision or problem.

You are a thinker; all human beings are thinkers. That is one important capability that makes us different from animals — we think!

More important, you are a good thinker. You may not believe this, but it is true. Most Americans do not get as far in school as you have. This is a sign that you think fairly well even if you are not aware of it.

To become even more skillful in your thinking you must become aware of your thoughts. You, as a human being, can do this. You can become conscious of your thoughts and mental activities. Animals as far as we know are not aware that they think. People like you can be aware of thought.

Consider professional ballplayers — centers in basketball, goalies in hockey, first basemen in baseball, or tight ends in football. Why are they professionals? Partly luck, partly mental attitude, but also partly awareness of their bodies.

We run, jump, turn. Professional ball players do too, but they are simultaneously very aware of their body movements. They are alert to the actions of their feet as they run, jump, or turn. They have studied how feet work and what happens when they move this way or that. They are aware.

Professional ball players have combined knowledge and actions in practice and in game situations. They have confronted something we all can do, become aware of it, learned about it, and made it part of a controlled consciousness. That is the key factor in becoming a professional ballplayer — conscious awareness of and control over the body.

As with the body, so with the mind. The mind acts for us when we need it, just like the body does. The actions of the body we call **movement.** The actions of the mind we call **thinking**.

We can become aware of, improve and control many actions of our minds like the actions of our bodies. We can become aware of our thinking, learn about it, improve it. We can control much of our thinking.

That is what this book is about. It is to help you become more aware of and in control of your thinking. Why is that important? It is important because a good student is usually a consciously thinking student. It is important because a worker with a good future is usually one who thinks and knows that he or she thinks. It is important because a good citizen is usually one who thinks things through and knows it. Careful, conscious thinking is something you can do. It is something that often makes the difference between success and failure. It is worth struggling and sweating for — to become a more successful student, worker, friend, family member, consumer and so forth. This book will help if you take it seriously, do the mental work which is asked of you, and most importantly record your mental actions. This is one book where it is indeed true that you will get out of it only as much as you put into it.

Most of this book will be exercises. You will be thinking, not just learning about thinking. This thinking is like playing baseball instead of reading about it. You will start the process by learning to do at least four things:

- ❑ Explain and give examples of why improving your conscious thinking skills will help you in personal, academic, and job situations.
- ❑ Identify and describe choices you have made.
- ❑ Use the technique of brainstorming to identify many alternative solutions to a choice.
- ❑ List and apply different methods of making choices.

Where do we start? The first step is to find out what thinking means. For the purposes of this book, we define it this way:

> **Thinking** means those conscious and unconscious mental skills we use when reacting to a choice.

There are five or six important words other than *Thinking* in that definition. What are they?

All of the situations listed at the beginning of this Introduction were choices: buying, college, relationships with others. When we face a choice, we deal with it. Sometimes we act **instinctively**, without much thought. Sometimes we think carefully for a long time. Sometimes we think some but not too much. But *we always think to some degree.*

Knowing that we think and knowing how we think are two very different things. We all use a certain group of mental skills when we think. All of us have them and use them. Unfortunately our mental skills are often like our physical ones — we use them without being aware of them. We run, laugh, gesture, unconscious of what our bodies are doing. We also think, decide and solve without being aware of what our minds are doing. Therefore, the first step in becoming alert to our thinking must be to learn about the mental skills that we all have and use.

What Are Thinking Skills?

- Thinking skills are tools for making decisions, solving problems, choosing.

- The better you are with thinking skills, the better you will be at making choices. Practice improves thinking just like it improves running.

- Thinking skills do not focus on your final decision as much as on how you decide. They relate to whether or not you know what you are doing, not to whether it comes out well. Experts and beginners can both burn cakes, take the wrong turn when driving, ruin something they are trying to fix, or say something stupid to a customer. The difference? Experts do this much less often because they are conscious of what they are doing and of what usually works. The same is true of expert thinkers and problem solvers.

- You already know how to use thinking skills in some ways. You use them every day even if you are not aware of it.

- You can improve your use of thinking skills if you know how, when and why you use them.

- Thinking is not an inborn ability that cannot be changed. Most thinking skills can be learned or polished through deliberate study and practice.

Why Are Thinking Skills Important?

- Employers say that a major difference between average employees and good ones is the ability to think things through, make decisions, solve problems. Learning to think better will clearly help you on the job.

- Thinking skills are also useful in your courses. They will help you understand and complete assignments, take tests, read carefully and do other things that help you succeed in college.

- Being aware that you are thinking will put you in control of your life. You will feel confident about yourself and what you can achieve.

- You think hundreds of times a day anyway; you cannot help it. You might as well learn to do it as well as possible.

- Making decisions is often difficult when you have few or no really good choices. Awareness of your thinking skills can help you deal with that difficulty.

How Will This Book Help Improve Your Thinking?

This is an unusual textbook. It does not concentrate on presenting material and then giving you things to memorize. It concentrates on helping you think and gives you things to do. What does that mean for you as you work on this book? These things:

- ❑ You will explore how you actually think in many school, work or personal situations.
- ❑ Your answers to questions about those situations will help you apply thinking skills to them.
- ❑ You will learn several specific thinking skills in detail and practice them in real world situations.
- ❑ You will discover some general thinking tools that help in all sorts of situations — skills you already use.
- ❑ You will combine individual, team and class activities; you will learn from other students and they will learn from you.
- ❑ You will learn by doing, thinking and discovering how and how well you already think.
- ❑ You will deal with many questions that do not have a right answer. The best answer will often depend on your ideas, values, explanations.

Exercise 1a

Brainstorming— A Way Of Thinking With A Group

Imagine a big thunderstorm with much thunder, and lightning bolts shooting in all directions. A lot of energy is being produced in the confusion of the storm.

One technique for group thinking is like a thunderstorm. It produces many bolts of ideas going in all directions. It is called **brainstorming**.

Brainstorming is a method of getting a group to respond quickly and productively to a question. It is a technique used often in this book. It is also a technique that is easy to learn and often fun to use.

To brainstorm, the class suggests as many ideas as they can. Everyone should speak up very rapidly in short sentences with little explanation. The goal is to generate as many ideas as possible, not to judge their worth.

Brainstorming has several important rules. They are designed to keep ideas coming without making judgements about their quality. Here are the rules:

- ❑ Never judge anyone's suggestions — do not criticize or comment on them.
- ❑ Work for quantity of ideas, not quality — the longer the list, the better you have brainstormed.
- ❑ Expand on each other's ideas — add to them, change them and make them different.
- ❑ Encourage far-out ideas — weird, funny and strange ideas are encouraged.

- ❑ Have someone record each idea — write down at least a key word or phrase.

- ❑ Set a time limit (usually 5-15 minutes) and stick to it.

When you use this technique, you generate many ideas — good, bad, or simply strange. First get a long list and then pick out the good possibilities.

Now try brainstorming. Your instructor will give you a topic in the form of a question. Follow the instructions below.

1. Write down the question:

2. List as many solutions as you can below.

3. Brainstorm as a class, following the six rules. Add to your separate page any class ideas which you especially like.

4. As a team, decide which ideas are best (be ready to define what you mean by "best") in that situation. Write them here.

5. Write down your comments on the brainstorming technique below.

Exercise 1b

Choice Situations—All Around Us, Always

When do we think? Simple: we think any time we are aware (consciously or unconsciously) that more than one choice exists. These are called **choice situations**, and we face them hundreds of times every day. Here are some examples:

- deciding to accept a job or quit one.
- picking a movie to see.
- responding when someone says, "Good morning. How are you?"
- deciding what to write for a big English paper.
- choosing a TV program to watch on Thursday night.
- figuring out what to say in a prayer.
- being asked to a party when you should study for a test.
- wanting to sleep when the kids need your attention.
- taking a position on an article you just read.
- accepting or refusing a cup of coffee or cigarette.
- deciding what to do when the car breaks down on the road.
- picking a route to take to work in the morning.
- wondering whether or not to ask for further instruction on an important assignment.
- reacting to a yellow light as you get to a corner.
- ordering a meal at McDonald's.

How about you? Think about how often you think through a situation, even if you do not notice that you are doing so. Think back and answer these questions:

1. List five choices you have made in the last 24 **hours.**

2. List five significant choices you have made in the past **week.**

3. List five important choices you have made in the past **year.**

4. What is the total number of choices you have made in the last 365 days, including very minor choices? Write a number here and then compare answers with others in the class.

Exercise 1c

Three Types Of Choices We Make

Each of us makes choices in different ways. We make choices differently when tired than when rested, rushed or relaxed. We make choices differently in class than at home, and we make school decisions differently than we do personal decisions. We make choices differently when we are very familiar with a subject than when it is new to us. We make very important choices in a different way than we make everyday choices.

Let's look at the differences in our choices by answering the questions below. One example is given for each question. Try to list two or three other answers that could be true for you.

1. What choices do you make differently in private than in front of your friends?

    a. *To cry or yell (or not) when something goes wrong.*

    b.

    c.

2. What choices do you make differently when you are happy than when you are depressed?

    a. *To chat with your friends or not.*

    b.

    c.

3. What choices do you make differently among friends than among strangers?

    a. *To say what you think about another person.*

    b.

    c.

Have you ever worried greatly about something that was not important at all? Have you ever made a quick, off-the-cuff decision and then discovered that you should have spent more time thinking it over? All of us have done these things and usually regretted it later.

Wise thinkers match the effort with the importance of the choice. Some choices deserve a lot of time and thought; other choices do not. Your thinking will be strongest when you can match importance with effort.

One way to do this is to first decide how important the choice is. How much of your time and attention does it deserve? An ordinary, familiar choice does not merit much effort. A very important or unfamiliar choice may demand that you think quite a bit. First identify the size of the choice. Then give it just as much attention as it deserves, but no more.

One way to look at this issue is to divide all choices into three types: **impulsive** choices, **habitual** choices and **systematic** choices. The three types differ in terms of the effort that goes into making them. Understanding and using these three types of choices will help you think skillfully.

Impulsive Choices

Most of our daily choices are impulsive ones. This means that we make a decision without thinking much about it. We follow our impulse in choosing what feels good or right.

Examples of impulsive choices might be:

- deciding what cereal to eat this morning.
- buying those special jeans because your friend does.
- picking a seat in a class on the first day.
- buying orange juice instead of milk.
- walking down one hall instead of another.
- making a comment in a conversation.

Making choices impulsively makes life bearable. There are too many daily choices; we cannot spend much mental effort on most of them. We would go crazy trying to think all of them through carefully. We would be very dull companions.

On the other hand, if too many of our choices are made impulsively we may have a different problem. We may miss opportunities, bore frequently, fail to grow, or create other problems for ourselves. Even worse, we may in effect turn our lives over to other people. Impulsive choices are valuable ways of making minor choices, but they can outgrow their appropriate role if we are not careful.

Habitual Choices

Habitual choices are those based on our habits. We do something today because we did it yesterday or because it is the thing to do. We may give some thought to the choice, but mostly we follow our usual pattern or rut.

Examples of habitual choices would be to *always* do these things:

- follow a certain route to work each day.
- regularly put on certain combinations of clothes.
- pick up the newspaper as soon as we get home from work.
- wait hand and foot on our spouse and children.
- buy the regular brand of peanut butter or milk.
- stop when we see the light turn red.
- sit in the same seat all term in a course.

Making such choices out of habit can be very valuable. Our habit of stopping when the light turns red has a very sound basis — it can save our life. Sometimes habitual choices are simply convenient; picking up one brand of peanut butter saves us the hassle of comparing all the brands every time. Sometimes habitual choices are simply practical; having habits in what we wear allows us to get five extra minutes of sleep.

But we can overdo our habitual choices. If we never question our habits, we may never discover that we have changed. We may never realize that our tastes are now different, that we have new potential interests, or that we have emerging abilities. We need to reexamine our habits occasionally and reassess the choices we make habitually.

What is the difference between **impulsive** and **habitual** choices?

What do **impulsive** and **habitual** choices have in common?

When is **choosing a classroom seat** an impulsive choice and when is it a habitual choice?

Systematic Choices

Systematic choices are those which require us to pay attention and think carefully. Some examples of choices that *should* be systematic are the following:

- getting married or divorced.
- moving to a new home.
- choosing or changing a job.
- buying a new car.
- resisting a very exciting temptation.
- voting.
- dealing with a major course assignment.
- choosing to go to or stay in college.

Some systematic choices are not big or important but unfamiliar: for example, operating a machine for the first time. We need to pay attention and proceed carefully; we are not sure of what we are doing. Before we press a button we need to think systematically about what might happen.

Many of us try to avoid systematic choices. We do not face them very often. We do not like to think carefully or hard; it seems unfamiliar. Therefore we try to rely on impulse or habit ("I'll do this because it feels right," or "Let's do that and get it over with!").

Systematic choices require us to have some conscious idea of how to solve a problem or make a decision. We need a **system** — a set of methods we can understand and use. People with such a system of thinking are better armed to deal with life than those who do not have such a system. They have a better chance of controlling their fate and their future. Systematic thinking is like a spare tire or an insurance policy. We need it in more situations than we imagine.

There is one final thing to realize about systematic choices; they do **not** have to take a lot of time. Your mind can work very quickly, and often you can make a difficult choice systematically in only a few seconds. On the other hand you can spend hours agonizing over a familiar choice and then **still** make it impulsively or habitually. The length of time you spend thinking is not always related to how you eventually make the choice.

Now identify the difference between **systematic choices** and the other two types:

1. Can you identify the three types of choices? Many choices were listed at the beginning of the previous exercise: impulsive, habitual and systematic. Decide what each type of choice is for you personally. Then discuss your answers with others in the class, defending your labels if necessary.

2. Below, write down at least two things you learned through those class discussions of types of choices.

3. All of us make systematic, habitual and impulsive choices. List four of each type of choice that you have made during the last week. Be specific about the choice.

    a. Four **impulsive** choices I made during the past week were:

    b. Four **habitual** choices I made during the past week were:

    c. Four **systematic** choices I made during the past week were:

    d. Share your answers with the class and discuss them.

Exercise 1d

Making Choices: A Range of Possibilities

Consider the difference between these two questions:

- What is the sum of 12 and 15?
- What is a number larger than 26?

One clear difference between the questions is the number of possible answers. The number 27 could be the right answer for both. However, for the first question 27 is the only right answer. The second question has millions of right answers in addition to 27. Look at these two choices:

- What should I do this weekend?
- Should I study or party tonight?

The first question allows many answers since you will probably do many things. The second one allows few answers: study, party or both. Some of our choices allow many answers. Some allow few. Some allow only one right answer. You can best make choices if you can estimate the number of answers available.

Buying drinks is an example of the difference.

- You are going to buy either a Coca-Cola or a 7-Up (the only two choices) from a machine,

  or

- You are going to buy something to drink for your family at the grocery store.

In the first situation you have only two choices. In the second you have many choices, and you must also consider your family's tastes as well as your own.

Choices with few answers often let you focus right away on basic information, values, and outcomes. You do not have to worry about sorting choices first; you can think immediately about the relative "rightness" of specific choices.

Choices with many answers may demand different thinking skills or patterns. You may spend most of your mental energy trying to balance combinations of possible answers instead of finding one "right" answer.

Your mental activities are probably more efficient if you determine how many reasonable answers the choice gives you, and then use that information to decide how to attack the choice. You can then best decide what specific techniques to use in making the choice, since the best thinking techniques for many-answered and few-answered choices often differ.

1. See if you can find the difference between "many-answered" and "few-answered" choices. Below are listed ten choices, some with many and some with relatively few answers. Put a checkmark before those you think are "many-answered."

    a. What cereal is the best-tasting?

    b. What is the smallest country in the world?

    c. For what job should I apply after I graduate?

    d. Why is water important for living?

    e. What cereal in this store costs the least?

    f. Should I try to get a job as a teacher's aide or as a social worker?

    g. What should I say or do when someone says "Do you want a cola?"

    h. What should I say or do when I hear that the professor thinks I cheated on the test?

    i. What country is smaller than the United States?

    j. How do oxygen and hydrogen mix in order to create water?

Compare answers with others in your class and try to agree as a *team* on which ones are many-answered. Be ready to explain your conclusions.

With other students, decide which questions were hard to categorize as many-answered or few-answered and *why* they were hard. List your answers and reasons below.

Finally, discuss this question: How do you know whether a question has few or many answers? Write your answers here.

Clue: What clues do you find in the questions themselves?

Often when we have decisions to make and problems to solve, we limit our possibilities by taking a narrow view of the question facing us. The way we pose the question often limits the number of possible solutions. When we take an either/or position, a black/white, right/wrong position, we may be shutting out some potentially good choices.

2. Consider the question below as a team, imagining yourself to live in a drafty house with primitive heating. Imagine the situation, then answer the question:

   What can I do about the poor heat
   in winter at the place where I live?

   The team's task is to identify as many alternatives as possible in this situation and then to decide what alternative to choose (and why).

   a. What answers can you think of?

   b. Which answer is best, and why?

   c. Was this a "few-answered" or a "many-answered" question?

      Explain your reason.

   d. How did you think this problem through? What mental processes did you use?

3. Here is another question to consider. Again, think of as many alternatives as you can and pick the best. Imagine that you are a new college student asking yourself this question.

   In what program of study should I enroll at this school?

   a. List as many possible answers as you can.

   b. Which is the "best" answer and why?

   c. Is this a "few-answered" or a "many-answered" question?

   d. Did you tackle this problem differently in your mind than you did the previous one about the heat in the apartment? If so, describe how your approach differed.

Homework

Write down on a separate sheet at least five times when you had a choice with many answers. Do not use something too simple, such as the number of different sandwiches to choose from in a restaurant. List complicated things. Include the situation and the alternatives you could identify.

Chapter Two

Tools For Thinking

We are best equipped if we fill our mental toolboxes with a few carefully chosen, broadly useful thinking tools.

We all think, but some of us seem to think better than others. No two people think exactly alike. A method for thinking or problem-solving that fits you may not fit your friends, for our strengths and weaknesses vary. Some of us are very good at one thing, others at another. Some of us approach a problem one way, others in a different way.

There is one thing, however, we all do; we use mental tools to help us think and solve problems. We have all been given a tool kit for thinking — a set of tools and procedures to use when we face a problem or decision. Many of us are not conscious that we use these tools, but all of us do.

Having a set of natural mental tools and using them to the utmost, however, are two different things. One of the things that education is supposed to do is make you aware of your mental tools and then help you learn how to use them skillfully. Unfortunately, some schools do not see this as a priority. All too often we have been asked to memorize facts and procedures with no time left for the process of thinking and learning. A major goal of the exercises in this book is to make sure that you are conscious of and skillful with the mental tools you use to think, solve problems, and make choices. The first step in the process must be to become aware of those mental tools you are using. Next, you will add to them and improve your use of them.

As you improve your thinking skills, you must observe yourself — pinpoint the actions of your mind as you think something through. It is like stop-frame action on TV — when a single shot is frozen you can suddenly see things you missed before. To improve your thinking, you have to learn to freeze a single thought or mental activity so that you know it is there and what it feels like. Only then can you analyze it and learn to control it.

Focusing on how you arrive at an answer or a solution is difficult at first because it requires you to move your attention away from the "right answer" and toward the process or mental strategies you use to get there. Often you may say, "I don't know how I got my answer; I just know the answer." The question now, however, is "How did you know the answer?" You must focus on the sequence of thinking that produces that answer. In the beginning this is not easy, but with practice you will be able to identify the Thinking Tools you are using.

You may find that sometimes you draw a blank. You cannot think of anything. Perhaps your mind refuses to work because you are in a new situation or feel anxious. Perhaps someone once told you, wrongly, that you were not good at thinking or problem solving, and you foolishly believed her or him. Our past experience has enormous influence on how and whether we tackle new situations, as well as on our confidence in ourselves as thinkers. As you become more conscious of your mental tools, your reluctance to tackle new problems should occur less often. You will feel more confident about unknown or unfamiliar situations.

Let us look at these thinking tools we all have and use.

Try This Problem $5 + 3 + 2 = ?$

How do you solve that problem?

Stop!

What is happening in your mind right now?

Are you thinking about this problem?
___ yes ___ no

If you answered *yes* to that question, you are somewhat aware of your mental activity. If you answered *no* you simply have not yet noticed how busy your mind is. Try another question:

- What is your left leg doing right now? Is it tense, relaxed, bent, straight?

- What is your mind doing right now? Is it anxious, buzzing with ideas, curious?

- What is your right shoulder doing right now?

- What is your mind doing right now?

Did you become aware of your body and mind? Usually we take our bodies and minds for granted. We do not notice that parts of our body are moving, tense, or at rest. If it is hard to notice the movements of our body, think how much harder it is to notice the movements of our mind.

Yet both our bodies and our minds are almost always active — doing something. Experts who study the relationship between body and mind tell us that the two are always moving in reaction to each other. Our mind worries; our arms become tense in reaction. Our eyes move and dilate; our mind becomes alert in reaction. *Our body and mind are continually interacting as they face choices.* This does not mean that something will always be going wrong. It simply means that we are alive: continually facing new and different experiences.

How have we learned to deal with continual change over the years? Our bodies have learned to run, throw, hit, manipulate, stroke. Our minds have learned to consider alternatives, try out ideas, draw mental pictures, weigh risks. To tune up our physical reactions, we must become sensitive to our bodies' activities and responses. To tune up our mental reactions, we must become sensitive to our minds' tools.

This is not easy, but it is important.

Think about coming to a major intersection when you are on a trip. You might think of many things — how much gas you need, if you are hungry, whether you need to go to the bathroom, your tiredness, the traffic patterns, the place you are going, and the alternative routes. You face not one but many choices.

Your decision at the intersection is reached unconsciously. Many factors, however, went into your decision, considered and eliminated in a very short time because thinking occurs very rapidly. A Thinking Tool you most likely would use is "Consider my alternatives." Another might be "Eliminate those things you don't want to do." A third would be to think of the consequences — "What might happen if I tried to pull over right here?"

How do you deal with the mental parts of those choices? Everyone does the same thing. We reach into our tool kit of thinking skills, pull out some tools, and use them. Throughout our lives we have unconsciously collected a set of Thinking Tools. We have learned to use them in certain habitual ways. And we do.

Do you notice a similarity between those last statements and what you learned in the previous chapter about the three types of choices? For many of us, our use of Thinking Tools is habitual or impulsive — we are not much in control of what we think or decide. A major goal of this book is to help you use your mental tools consciously and systematically when you need to do so.

The first, most important step is to help you recognize the powerful Thinking Tools in your mind. You may not be very certain that you have a mental Thinking Tool Kit, much less of its contents. In this chapter and others we will try to help you discover the contents of that tool kit. We will try to help you identify your Thinking Tools and then improve your ability to use them to meet your needs.

This chapter is about Thinking Tools. In it you will learn to do at least the following three things:

- ❑ Identify general Thinking Tools you use to solve personal, career, or academic problems;
- ❑ Distinguish between broad Thinking Tools and narrow Thinking Rules; and
- ❑ Explain and give examples of how Thinking Tools are useful in solving problems.

Although this specific chapter concentrates on Thinking Tools, you will also find them in the rest of the book. Remember the questions a few pages ago which were surrounded by a box like this:

Any Time You See This,
Get Ready
For **Thinking Tools**

These boxes are like flashlights. They shine on moving objects in your mental dark. When you see these boxes try to spot thinking going on in your head.

The boxes are one aid to you in becoming familiar with your mental processes. Another key to Thinking Tools is in the other students in your class. Explain your thinking to them and listen to their explanations of their thinking. You will be surprised at how often other students describe a thinking technique they use — and you realize you use it also.

To use the boxes effectively you must write in them. Record the Thinking Tools you and the other students discover. As you crystallize your ideas into words and phrases, write them in the boxes.

Since thinking is active, not passive, your Thinking Tools should also be active statements that describe the actions of your mind; they should begin with verbs. Use action words like consider, look at, gather, ask, put, take.

Exercise 2a

Thinking About Toothpicks

Most of this book deals with Thinking Tools in personal, career, or school situations. However, it is perhaps easier to begin identifying Thinking Tools as we solve puzzles. Below are a figure and a question. Try to solve the problem, but at the same time try to become aware of the activities of your mind. How are you trying to solve the problem? What actions are you taking in your mind? The purpose of this exercise is not to solve the problem; it is to begin identifying Thinking Tools.

Problem

The figure below is made of 13 toothpicks which make four equal-sized squares. Remove only one toothpick and make three equal-sized squares.

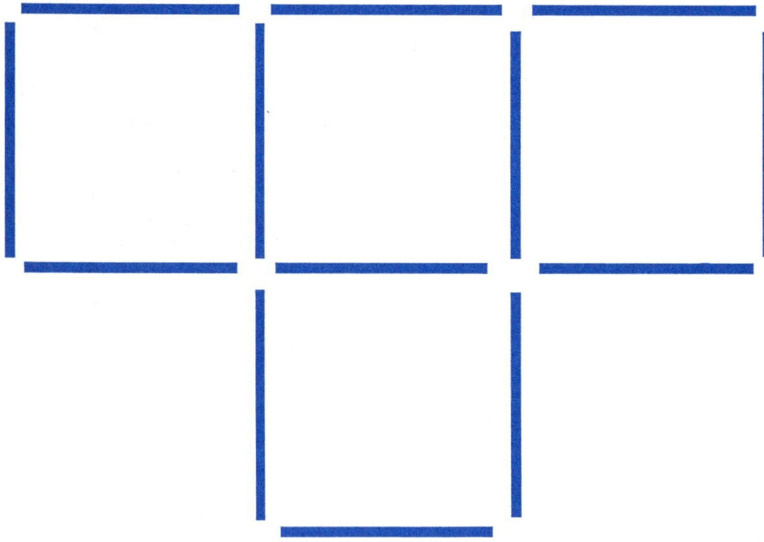

As you try to solve this problem, write down anything you can identify concerning the actions of your mind. What are you thinking about? How are you breaking down and tackling the problem? Your mind is doing something to solve this problem. What is it?

•

•

•

•

•

•

When you have completed the problem and made notes of your ideas, share your ideas concerning your mental activities with others in the class. As you do that, you will find that others also have very good insights into their thinking.

Write down any ideas they suggest that you used but simply did not become aware of.

•

•

Exercise 2b

Practicing The Thinking Tool Of Finding Alternatives

An important Thinking Tool is the ability to **think of alternatives.** In most problems or decisions, our natural desire is to think of our choices: our alternative courses of action. We use our minds to imagine different possibilities.

This is a tool which is effective in job, school or personal situations. It fits many choices or decisions. It is a basic Thinking Tool that you should place very close to the top of your kit of Thinking Tools. This exercise will help you make it one of your most valuable and most-used tools. Imagine yourself in each of these situations and answer the questions fully and thoughtfully.

1. Imagine you hear that a good friend of yours has been thrown out of school for cheating.

   a. Right now describe what you are thinking in reaction to this situation. What ideas are you considering, and what is your mind doing with them?

   b. You probably thought of several alternative explanations for the above situation. List as many of them as you can.

c. What conclusion did you reach concerning this rumor?

d. List at least one way in which your Thinking Tools helped you reach that conclusion.

e. Compare your answers with those of other students.

2. Imagine that you won $1,275 in a sweepstakes.

   a. Write down your immediate mental reaction to this situation. What occurred to you? What did you consider? What did you reject, accept? How did your mind do that? Write down as much as you can about your mental processes.

   b. List at least six ways to use the money that you actively considered.

c. What did your mind do with the alternatives as they occurred to you? For example, you probably compared each alternative to the sum of $1,275 to see if there was enough money for that choice. What else did your mind do with the alternatives?

d. Which alternative did you like best and why?

e. As you finish this part of the exercise, compare your answers with others in the class. List here any things they came up with that you realize your mind did also.

3. Imagine that, in your English class, you are assigned to write a one or two page essay on this topic: the most important thing that has ever happened to me.

   a. What possibilities do you think about? List at least four.

   b. What actions was your mind taking while you thought about this situation?

4. The previous activities ask you to imagine yourself in three different situations. Can you compare those situations in terms of the range of alternatives and the difficulty of choosing among them?

   a. The situation of how to interpret the news of a friend being thrown out of school was:

   b. The situation of deciding how to spend sweepstakes winnings was:

   c. The situation of deciding what to write in an English paper was:

5. Often, when faced with a choice, we take a narrow view of the situation and therefore fail to see other alternatives. For example, someone who discovers that his car will need very expensive repairs before it will run well enough to get him to school might decide that the choice was this:

   Should I get the car fixed and keep going to school or quit school?

   Consider the difference in alternatives if we focus not on the issue of getting the car fixed but on the issue of going to school. Here is another way to phrase that question:

   How can I arrange to get back and forth to school each day?

There is evidence that our minds tackle problems differently depending on whether they are few-answered or many-answered. You discussed that in the previous chapter. You can see the difference when you think through the two alternative questions on the previous page. Read the following descriptions carefully, and see if you can recognize similarities between them and the way your mind acts in these situations.

- "With the first question, there seemed to be only two choices: yes or no. My mind seemed to move inward towards those two choices and to bounce off them the consequences of choosing one or the other. I kept bouncing *cost* and *college degree* and *hassle* and other factors off of the two alternatives. It was sort of like throwing different substances against two different types of walls (a *yes* wall and a *no* wall) to see how they bounced differently."

- "With the second choice, I felt that there were probably many possibilities. My mind seemed to move *outward* towards finding more and more possibilities. I thought of friends who could drive me, and that led me to think about fellow students in my classes even if they weren't close friends. Somehow I seemed to keep looking outwards towards more possibilities and was less interested in bouncing things like *cost* and *college degree* against my choices than I was in finding *new* choices that might suit me even better."

Discuss these two descriptions with your class. See how many students also identify some qualitative differences in how they use Thinking Tools with few-answered versus many-answered questions.

6. This final activity once again encourages you to become sensitive to how your mental processes occur. In the previous activity you explored how your mind might treat alternatives differently with broad or narrow questions. You discussed it with the class. Now practice using that kind of insight once again, with different questions. Please follow these directions **exactly**.

Deal with the following questions one at a time. One is narrow and one broad. Cover the second question (the one below the dotted line) with a sheet of paper, so that you can concentrate fully on how your mind grapples with the first question.

Imagine that you are just entering college and are being asked to identify the program of study that you want to pursue.

Question 1

Do I want to major in computer programming?

Instructions

Become aware of how your mind is using alternatives as a tool in trying to answer this question. Make some notes here.

Question 2

What kind of work do I want to do in my life?

Instructions

Become aware of how your mind is grappling with alternatives in this situation. Make some notes here.

Did you identify any differences in how your mind used the Thinking Tool of identifying alternatives with the two different types of questions? Discuss this with others in the class.

Exercise 2c

Thinking Through Giving A Party

Imagine that you have just received a phone call and learned that a very special friend will be in town two days from now. You want to give a party for your friend. It will be a fairly large party and you only have two days to prepare for it!

1. What goes on in your mind as you try to deal with this idea? Do not list the things you will do (such as invite people, buy food, or find a place). Do list the ways your mind goes about thinking the problem through. What Thinking Tools are you using? List some here (two examples are given).

   - *Make a mental list of people to invite.*
   - *Imagine what your friend would enjoy.*
   -
   -
   -

2. After you make your own list of Thinking Tools explore the actual steps you would take in planning that party — what you would do. List them on a separate sheet. As you do this, be aware of your mental processes.

3. See if you can add at least one Thinking Tool based on what happened as you answered the second question. What were you doing in your mind? Discuss it with others and see if you can add at least one other Thinking Tool to your list.

Exercise 2d

Thinking Through Giving Directions

In this situation imagine you are giving someone directions to your home from where you are right now.

1. What goes through your mind when you think about this situation? Do not list the actual directions (the roads, turns, landmarks, etc.). Instead, as a class, suggest the mental processes you are using. Your instructor will record what the class suggests. You may want to write those Thinking Tools here. One example is given.

    - *Visualize what each turn looks like.*
    -
    -
    -
    -
    -
    -

2. Pair off with another student and tell that person how to get to your house. As you do so, be aware of mental activities. When you finish, answer this question: were you using the Thinking Tools listed above?

3. Finally, add any other Thinking Tools to the list you made above. Discuss the exercise and your list with your partner. See if together you can come up with additional Thinking Tools.

Exercise 2e

Thinking Rules Versus Thinking Tools

Think about working as an automobile mechanic. There are surely 2,000 different instruments that you could use when fixing different parts of a car. Could you afford to buy all of them? Could you carry them around if you did buy them? Obviously not. They would cost and weigh too much.

What, then, do auto mechanics do? They buy a few tools that are very flexible and can be used in many situations. Those few tools may be a little less easy to use in specific situations, but they can handle almost all the jobs of the 2,000 specialized tools. They are cheaper and light enough to carry around in a tool kit.

Think about some other tools. A scout knife has more uses than a surgeon's scalpel. Both cut, but the scout knife cuts many more things and is far more sturdy than a delicate scalpel. Both a shovel and a power edger can trim grass at the edge of a driveway, but a shovel can also be used for many other things. A one-half teaspoon measure is useful only for measuring exactly one-half teaspoon of salt, spices, or other ingredients. A two-cup measuring cup with gradations on the side, however, can measure many different quantities. Each is a tool, but some are more broadly useful than others.

This principle also applies to Thinking Tools. There are thousands of specialized techniques for dealing with specific problems, but a few properly chosen Thinking Tools can do the job of almost all of them. Your mathematics instructor can solve so many different types of problems not because she or he has thousands of specialized mental tools, but because she or he knows how to use a few general Thinking Tools. The same is true for any good teacher, any expert, or anyone who is good at thinking things through.

Your mind is your mental toolbox and like the automobile mechanic's physical toolbox it has limited capacity. There is clear research evidence that each of us can remember and use only a very limited amount of information at one time. If you try to remember everything, you will spend almost all of your active mental capacity trying to recall specialized information into your conscious memory. You will not have any mental capacity left over to do anything with the information. You are therefore best equipped for thinking if you fill your mental toolbox with a few flexible Thinking Tools instead of with many specific methods limited to solving one kind of problem.

We will call the narrow, specialized technique for solving one certain type of problem a **Rule**. We will call the broad, flexible technique for tackling many different problems a **Tool**. Think about the difference when you look at the six items below.

____ a. Tagamet is a prescription drug used for treating ulcers.

____ b. An aspirin is a nonprescription drug used to relieve a headache, pain and other symptoms.

____ c. A pacemaker is a piece of electronic equipment used to regulate the heart.

____ d. A bandage is a piece of plastic and gauze used to cover small wounds.

____ e. Conditioner is a lotion used to soften hair.

____ f. Soap is a solid lotion used to clean or sterilize people, animals and things.

If you could only pack three of these items for a long family trip, which would be the most generally useful for everyone?

Remember that we said Rules are narrow and limited ways of thinking while Tools are broader, more flexible and more useful ways of thinking. The six items on the previous page are in some ways physical counterparts of Rules and Tools. The six items are in three pairs of similar items, one narrower (like a Thinking Rule) and one broader (like a Thinking Tool). See if you can match them up.

	Broader Item (Like a Tool)	**Narrower Item** (Like a Rule)
Pair # 1:		
Pair # 2:		
Pair # 3:		

How do we know the difference between a thinking rule and a thinking tool? Mostly it is a matter of habit, training and instinct. You have the basic ability to separate a Thinking Rule from a Thinking Tool, but you will need to practice and polish that skill in order to become an expert. Here are a few clues that might help:

- If a technique for thinking does not refer only to a specific situation, it is probably a tool.
- If a technique for thinking works in academic, job and personal situations (instead of in just one of them) it may be a tool.
- See if you can create a common-sense sentence when you add a technique for thinking after this phrase: "When in doubt, ..."

Following are some examples of techniques for thinking. Use the clues given above (especially the phrase "When in doubt ...") to decide which are thinking rules (narrow) and which are thinking tools (broad). Place an R or a T in front of each of them.

___ a. divide by the multiplier.

___ b. check your work.

___ c. double the salt.

___ d. increase the amount.

___ e. multiply length times width.

___ f. use a formula.

Do you see any difference in these items? Are some broadly useful with personal, career, and school situations? Are some narrowly useful only in specific situations?

The six items are actually three pairs. Items a and b, items c and d, and items e and f are pairs. In each case, the first item is narrower — it is a rule. Items a, c, and e are narrow rules; they only work in certain situations. They do not make a great deal of sense when added after the phrase, *When in doubt, ...* The other three items are broader versions of the same idea. Items b, d, and f are tools.

For example, *When in doubt, divide by the multiplier* is not very useful in most situations. It is a rule that you use to check your work after multiplying numbers. But *When in doubt, check your work* is much broader. It applies to mathematics, English, jobs, cutting grass, and other things. It is a broad, general Thinking Tool.

Following are some statements. Put an "R" before the ones that are narrow rules. Put a "T" before the ones that are broader tools.

a. Atlanta, Georgia is marked on a map by a star in a circle.

b. Follow directions.

c. Use symbols.

d. Round off your answer to the hundredths.

e. Find another word that means the same thing as "trash."

f. Look for commonalities or similarities.

g. If a word problem asks for the total amount, you should add.

h. Don't tackle every problem the same way.

i. Show your work in a math problem.

j. Use symbols and figures when working something out.

k. Use i before e, except after c, or when the sound is "a" as in neighbor or weigh.

l. Look for patterns.

Now, in your own words, describe the differences between a Thinking Rule and a Thinking Tool.

Earlier in this chapter, in exercises 2C and 2D, you listed a number of mental activities which you thought were Thinking Tools — thought processes you identified while solving a problem. Go back to those exercises now. Put an "R" (rule) or a "T" (tool) before each of them.

a. How many did you think were narrow rules, and how many were broad tools?

____ Tools ____ Rules

b. Discuss your judgements with others in your class. They probably disagree on some of the items. Discuss them for as long as you need to in order to get a solid grasp of Thinking Tools versus Thinking Rules.

By this point you have probably realized that one problem with distinguishing between Thinking Rules and Thinking Tools is that they are relative. A rule can be narrow yet still broader than something else. It is like the wedge below, very broad on one end (Tool) and very narrow on the other (Rule). Most mental techniques are somewhere between, like the *x,* but closer to one end than the other.

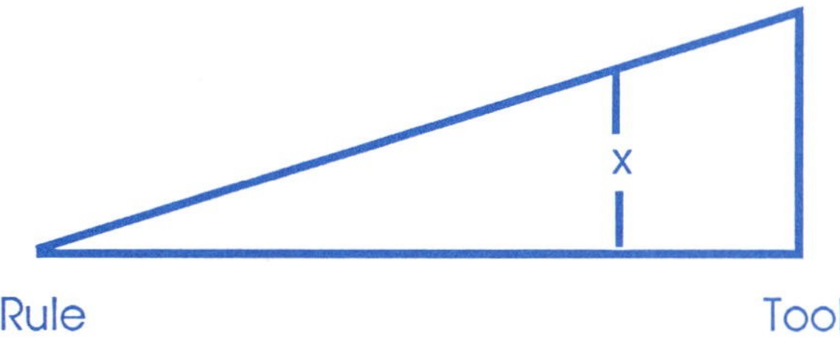

This is a matter of degree of generality. Some of the rules you listed could in fact become tools. How? By making them more general.

Analyze a rule such as *multiply length times width.* It is a narrow rule, useful only for determining the area of a rectangle. Can we make it broader? We can do so by asking, "What is it an example of?" It is one example of a formula for mathematical calculations. We might use that broader idea, and restate it as *use a formula. Use a formula* is much broader and fits many more situations than does the original statement of *multiply length times width.* A rule has become a tool.

See if you can apply this technique. If you decided that any of your mental activities in the previous exercises were actually Thinking Rules, try to change them into tools by making them more general. See if you can rewrite those rules so that they easily apply to many situations. For example, if in the exercise on giving directions you wrote down *see the red light at the turnoff* and now realize that it is actually a narrow rule, turn it into a broader tool such as *visualize the situation.* If you cannot transform all of the rules into tools, do not worry about it. This is difficult, and we have just begun working on Thinking Tools.

Exercise 2f

Using Thinking Tools In Personal Situations

Here is a personal situation that many people face: what to do about an ailing relative.

Read the situation and think it through, but focus on Thinking Tools as you did earlier. Pinpointing your mental techniques is the purpose of this exercise; your solution to this situation is less important.

> Your 55-year-old uncle lives with you. This morning he had a severe reaction to a medication. He is unconscious and may have major brain damage. His physical functions are failing. Your family doctor believes that your uncle will die unless placed on very specialized and expensive equipment within 24 hours.
>
> Your doctor doubts your uncle will regain consciousness but recalls a similar case wherein partial recovery occurred after three years. You are in school, working fulltime, and have a young child. Your parents and other relatives have historically been of little help during emergencies but quick to judge the actions of others who do try to help.

Think about this situation for a few minutes, concentrating on your mental activities. Then answer the following questions.

1. What questions came to mind while you were thinking through this situation? List the questions or ideas you considered.

2. What action(s) would you take in this situation with the uncle? Write down what you would do and discuss your choice.

3. What other information would you like to have before you make a choice? List the information here and where you would get it.

4. Now list the Thinking Tools you were aware of using while you thought through the situation. It may help to ask yourself what process you used to think up the ideas and questions you listed above, and what you then did with them in your mind once you had them.

-
-
-
-

5. Share your list of Thinking Tools with a team or the class. Listen to the ones they list. Now go back and add any of their Thinking Tools that you realize you use, too.

Exercise 2g

Thinking Through Another Toothpick Puzzle

Early in this chapter you tried to solve a puzzle which required you to move toothpicks in a certain pattern. You also had to be aware of your mental processes as you struggled with the puzzle. Below is a final toothpick puzzle and two questions.

Problem

Below is a shape made from twelve toothpicks. Your task is to move exactly four toothpicks in order to make three equal squares.

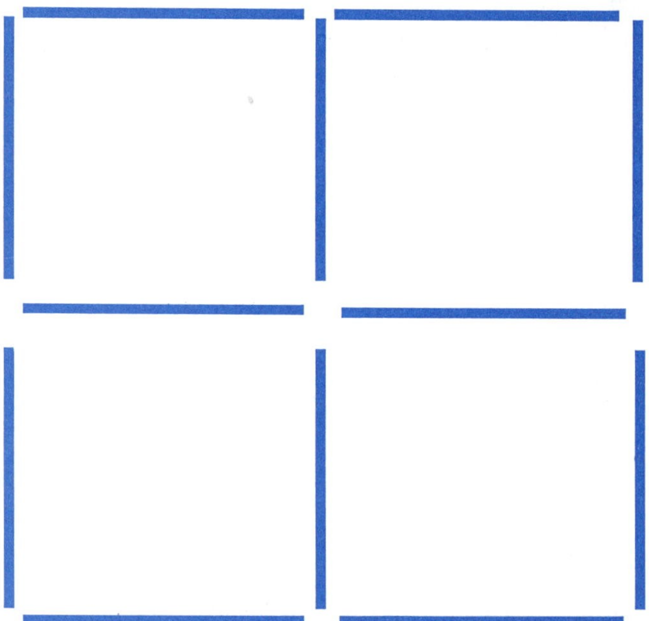

1. Try to solve this puzzle while concentrating also on the Thinking Tools you are using. Note below the Thinking Tools you find yourself using.

2. What is the solution to this problem? Draw it below.

3. Finally, think back to how difficult it was to become aware of your Thinking Tools in the earlier toothpick exercise. How much easier was it this time, and why? Discuss this with others in the class.

Exercise 2h

Pulling Together The Thinking Tools

You now have the beginnings of your thinking toolkit. In this chapter you have identified a number of Thinking Tools that you sometimes use. Your tools are probably very irregular in quality. Some are probably too general, too specific, or too vague. Some are probably clear, precise and powerful.

In this final activity in the chapter, you need to bring all of your Thinking Tools together. The space below is your initial toolbox. To fill it up do the following things:

Look through the exercises in this chapter and identify all the Thinking Tools you have found. Rewrite and refine the ones that seem most useful so that they are as clear, flexible, and useful as possible.

Then write the ones you have chosen and polished in the toolkit space.

My **Thinking Toolkit** Contains The Following Tools:

Chapter Three

Thinking In Patterns

We live, love, judge, learn, think, and act through the patterns which surround us. We need to find them, inspect them, and learn to use them consciously.

Patterns can be seen in all parts of our lives if we stop to think about them. Many things have patterns — seasons, weather, mealtimes, fashion trends, TV shows, behavior, and family activities, to name a few. We are constantly finding and making sense of patterns without realizing it. We do this instinctively. Making use of patterns can be important to success in school, on the job, or getting along with people.

In school, we have to be aware of patterns in our course work. For example, we need to recognize and use comparisons in reading, in writing, and in analyzing facts and concepts in any textbook. What do we compare in those situations? Usually we compare patterns.

We also use patterns in organizing paragraphs, essays, and research papers and in applying math or science formulas. Interpreting history, art, or literature is also much easier if we look for patterns.

On the job, we organize our work based on daily or weekly patterns. We solve problems by searching for patterns. Making management decisions often involves breaking decisions into parts, analyzing the parts, and seeing how they fit together. That is using patterns too. How does a good manager or machine operator know when a problem is developing in his or her work? Changes in the usual patterns often provide the main clue.

In our relationships with others we are influenced by changes in behavior patterns. If we see someone who is normally caring, open and relaxed suddenly not wanting to talk, edgy and generally irritable, we notice this change in pattern. Usually it indicates a problem or new situation of some type.

If we are sensitive to changes in normal patterns, we become more in tune with other people. Think about a good student who has always been interested and involved in school and has a nice set of friends. Suddenly she becomes moody and frequently ill, and begins skipping school. The change in pattern indicates a problem which needs to be analyzed by her family, friends, teachers, and counselors.

In this chapter you will learn how we find patterns by breaking down information into parts and discovering how the parts relate. You will learn to guess what the pattern might be and to figure out what the pattern really is. You have five objectives in this chapter:

- ❑ To recognize patterns in our personal lives, at school, and on the job.
- ❑ To recognize how patterns affect our actions and decisions.
- ❑ To predict behavior or events based on patterns.
- ❑ To identify and extend patterns in number sequences.
- ❑ To find some **Thinking Tools** for recognizing and using patterns when thinking through a situation.

Many of the activities in which we engage involve patterns of some type. We plan leisure time, chores, budget and work based on patterns. We use patterns when we work with numbers, whether we are solving a math problem or planning a party. We make predictions and forecasts based on number patterns (such as when our checkbook is lower than usual halfway through the month).

Think about different patterns at school, home, work and with friends.

Below, describe the patterns you can identify. Try to describe them well enough that others will be able to predict your actions.

1. One Pattern is:

2. One Pattern is:

3. One Pattern is:

4. One Pattern is:

5. One Pattern is:

6. One Pattern is:

7. One Pattern is:

Now look at those patterns you have just written down. Could someone else predict your actions based on what you wrote? If not, probably one (or both) of two things is wrong with them. Perhaps they are too short, general, and fuzzy (such as *I like to make a good impression*). You may have listed some topics instead of patterns.

- ❑ A **topic** is something like *my clothes* or *what I eat.* A topic names an aspect of your life.

- ❑ A **pattern** might be *I wear a suit to church on Sunday* or *I never eat breakfast.* A pattern describes what you usually do in that aspect of your life.

If you listed topics instead of patterns above, go back and change them. Now share the patterns you listed with others and discuss them.

Exercise 3a

Finding Patterns In Number And Letter Groups

One of the standard kinds of test items involves number and letter patterns. Number patterns look like this:

- 5, 10, 15, 20, 25, ___, ___, ___, ___, _?_

The question usually asks us to figure out what number to put in the "?" space.

To do that, we need to figure out what goes in the other spaces.

To do that, we need to figure out the number pattern.

We recognize this pattern easily because it is familiar. We habitually count by 5's.

See if you can figure out the pattern in this series of numbers; it is not a usual pattern.

- 1, 3, 2, 4, 3, 5, 4, 6, 5, ___, ___, ___, ___, _?_

How do you know what numbers come next? It helps to learn how others analyze the problem. Share your interpretation of the above pattern with others or learn their method if you could not find the pattern.

1. What is the pattern?

2. What number fits in the "?" space?

3. How did you know what the pattern was?

Here is another number series. Try to find the pattern, and write it down.

- 7, 10, 8, 11, 9, 12, 10, 13, ___, ___, ___, ___, _?_

Describe the pattern of the previous series.

How did you figure out what the pattern was? What mental activity was occurring as you wrestled with it?

Now try the following patterns. Fill in the numbers. Below each one, write a short description of the pattern so you can explain it to someone else.

1. 69, 63, 66, 65, 59, 62, 61, ____, ____, ____, ___

2. 42, 32, 64, 54, 108, 98, ____, ____, ____, ___

3. 20, 10, 40, 20, 80, 40, 160, ____, ____, ____, ___

4. 1, 2, 1, 4, 8, 7, 10, 20, ____, ____, ____, ___

Stop and share with others how you are making notes of the patterns. It is very frustrating to have to rediscover a pattern when you have forgotten it. Discuss the best way to note your patterns.

5. 6, 3, 4, 16, 8, 9, 36, ____, ____, ____, ___

6. 25, 5, 50, 10, 100, 20, 200, ______, ______, ______.______, ______

7. 8, 4, 10, 6, 12, 8, 14, ____, ____, ____, ___

8. 6, 18, 19, 15, 45, ____, ____, ____, ___

9. A, B, E, F, I, J ____, ____, ____, ___

10. C, G, E, I, G, K, ____, ____, ____, ___

Below, write down the system you would tell others to use if they wanted to solve **letter** pattern problems.

In case more practice would be useful, more number and letter problems are included in the supplementary exercises at the end of this chapter.

What **Thinking Tools** Are You Using With These Patterns?

Exercise 3b

Identifying Patterns In Daily Situations

Situations involving patterns occur constantly in our daily lives. Our ability to recognize them enables us to improve our reactions, plan our activities, and make better decisions. In the situations below you are asked to describe patterns; be specific when you state them.

Make sure that the pattern is clear enough for prediction. Again, do not simply state a topic. That does not help us predict or anticipate actions. For example, a topic might be *paying bills*, while a specific pattern might be *making the mortgage payment between the first and tenth day of every month.* The pattern lets us know what will happen in advance; the topic does not.

1. Al is sitting on a street corner waiting for his ride. He is early and starts watching the traffic light. It is a long, slow light. He starts timing how long the light is green and how long it is red. The light was green/yellow for 9:00. Here are the next colors of the light.

Red for	9:01-9:02.	Green/Yellow at	9:03.
Red for	9:04-9:05.	Green/Yellow at	9:06.
Red for	9:07-9:08.	Green/Yellow at	9:09.
Red for	9:10-9:11.		

Is there a pattern to the light? ____Yes ____No

If you answered *Yes*, what is the pattern?

Remember that patterns help us predict. What can you predict about the light? Will it be red (R), or green/yellow (G/Y) for the following times? Fill in R or G/Y.

9:13 _____ 9:15 _____ 9:17 _____

2. Now Al is at school. He is going to enroll at Pickle Community College and is trying to decide what to study. He is working with an advisor. He and the advisor look at his grades from the past. Here are some of Al's grades. They found a pattern. See if you can find it.

Course	Grade	Course	Grade
Physics I:	D	History:	A
Literature:	B	Physics II:	F
Algebra:	D	Composition:	A
Psychology:	A	Human Relations:	B
Electronics:	D	Chemistry:	D
Computer Science:	C	Government:	A

Is there a pattern? ____ Yes ____ No

If *Yes*, what is the pattern?

List three other courses in which you think Al would do well, based on the pattern you find.

List three other courses in which you think Al would do badly, based on that pattern.

We all have patterns, hidden sometimes in our grades and in the courses we like and do not like. What are your patterns of preferred courses? Below describe the pattern of your best and worst courses that an advisor might find when working with you.

Finally, what implications does your pattern of best and worst courses have for you in college? How can you use it to help you select courses and programs of study, seek tutoring, schedule studying? Write down some ideas about this question on a separate sheet and share them with someone else in your class.

3. Now look at Steve. Steve is in trouble at school because of poor grades, withdrawals from courses, and too many attendance problems. He and his advisor are trying to figure out what is happening, because Steve was previously a solid student. Here are some events in Steve's life over the past two weeks. See if there is a pattern.

Monday	Watched a three-hour TV special.
Tuesday	Got an A in accounting; went to a party.
Wednesday	Missed school; went to an evening movie.
Thursday	Got a B in data processing and a B in math; went out to a bar.
Friday	Got an F in English and a D in accounting.
Monday	Got an A in history; went to a party.
Tuesday	Got an F in English and did not do his homework in accounting and math; went to a long movie, then studied with his girlfriend.
Wednesday	Got a B in data processing and an A in accounting; went to a party.
Thursday	Cut school; went to the lake with friends at night.
Friday	Got an F in accounting; dropped the English course (failing).

Do you see any patterns? ____ Yes ____ No

If *Yes* what patterns do you see?

If you were the advisor, what would you discuss with Steve?

After enrolling in college your class schedule becomes a fixed pattern for the term. If you work, your working hours are also established as a fixed pattern. The time remaining is all you have for leisure activities, family, chores, studying, and sleep. It is important for you to establish and keep a general pattern of activities; otherwise, like Steve, your impulsive choices may well get the best of you.

On a separate sheet of paper analyze your patterns and set forth a plan of time use. Identify your fixed patterns. Estimate how much time you want or need to spend on each type of activity. Then fit it all together. Exchange your general plan with someone else in the class, and discuss the advantages and disadvantages of firming up such a pattern.

4. Mr. Gobbitt is vice-president for personnel with Applique Corporation. Here are his last seven hiring situations. In each case, he had three finalists, and the person he chose is in capital letters. Is there a pattern?

    a. Clerical Job: Mr. Granger, Ms. Lenti, MS. DARNELL

    b. Professional Job: Mr. Mandy, Ms. Ramirez, MR. TURNER

    c. Professional Job: Ms. Montgomery, MR. WRIGHT, Ms. Alex

    d. Clerical Job: MS. ABRAMS, Ms. Ho, Mr. Caldwell

    e. Clerical Job: MS. HO, Mr. Blackman, Ms. Gomez

    f. Professional Job: Ms. Bingham, MR. NORTH, Mr. Trent

    g. Professional Job: Mr. Lark, Ms. Samson, MR. YORK

    Do you see a pattern in who Mr. Gobbitt hires? ____ Yes ____ No

    If so, what is the pattern?

Following are Mr. Gobbitt's next two jobs to fill. Who do you predict he will hire? Circle your answer, then explain why.

h. Clerical Job: Ms. Candless, Mr. Millikan, Mr. McBee

Explanation:

i. Professional Job: Ms. Quick, Mr. Sullivan, Ms. Jacobs

Explanation:

If you were seeking a job with Applique Corporation, how would knowledge of Mr. Gobbitt's hiring patterns help you?

5. Gloria is the new assistant manager for a finance company. The daily mail is very important to her; she needs to know who has sent in what payments each day. She builds the office's daily work schedule around mail delivery.

After a few weeks on the job, she notices that sometimes the work schedule is smooth. Sometimes, though, it does not work — everyone has an easy morning but must rush all afternoon. Gloria starts tracking mail delivery to see if that has something to do with the problem. This is when the mail is delivered for three weeks.

Monday	11:15	Tuesday	11:03	Wednesday	12:10
Thursday	11:20	Friday	11:10	Saturday	12:30
Monday	11:07	Tuesday	11:19	Wednesday	12:22
Thursday	11:00	Friday	11:13	Saturday	12:15
Monday	11:17	Tuesday	11:17	Wednesday	12:19
Thursday	11:14	Friday	11:03	Saturday	12:38

a. Do you see a pattern? ____ Yes ____ No

b. If so, what is the pattern?

c. Suppose Gloria finds out that this summer there is a substitute mail carrier two days a week? Which two days do you think that person delivers the mail?

d. What do you think Gloria should do about this?

Identify at least two situations in your own life where you are dependent upon someone else's pattern.

Identify at least two situations where someone else is dependent upon your pattern.

Exercise 3c

Finding Patterns In Analogies

Intelligence tests, college entrance tests and job placement tests have analogy questions. What is an analogy? Here is one:

- Hub : Wheel :: Pupil : ________?

An analogy in this context is a word-set which shows relationships between words. Usually there is one pair (separated by one set of dots), two sets of dots, and then half of the second pair. You must decide what word belongs in the blank as the last half of the second pair.

How do we solve analogies? We often write them this way:

- Dawn : Dusk :: Day : ________?

And then we read them this way: "Dawn is related to dusk in the same way that day is related to what?" Dawn and dusk are one pair, and day is the first half of the second pair.

To solve the analogy, first discover the relationship between the first pair; what do dawn and dusk have in common? Dawn is the opposite of dusk, so the relationship might be that of opposites. What is the opposite of day? If night is given as a choice, then it is almost surely correct.

Relationship: Opposites

Let's look again at the first analogy in this exercise:

- Hub : Wheel :: Pupil: ________?

The hub is the center of a wheel. Of what is the pupil the center? Pupil can mean part of a class, so the correct answer might be "class." Pupil can also mean the center part of the eye, so the answer might be "eye." "Eye" seems to be a more appropriate answer, since the pupil is really not the center of the class in the same way that the hub is the center of a wheel. But either answer might be correct depending upon the choices given. The procedure is the same in either case. Figure out the pattern of the first pair and apply it to the second pair.

Here is another example:

- Home Run : Baseball :: Touchdown : ________?

What is the relationship in the first pair? A home run is a way to gain points in baseball. A touchdown is a way to gain points in what? Football, of course.

Relationship: points in games

For the analogies which follow, determine the pattern. Fill in the blank space after each analogy when you discover the pattern. Then, for each, explain how the two word pairs are related. You may use a dictionary to check the meaning of a word.

A. Examples:

1. Drill : Dentist :: Hammer: ________?

   Drill : Dentist :: Hammer: **Carpenter**

   Relationship: *A drill is used by a dentist, and a hammer is used by a carpenter.*

2. Wide : Narrow :: Deep : ________?

   Wide : Narrow :: Deep : **Shallow**

   Relationship: *Wide is opposite of narrow; deep is opposite of shallow.*

B. Write the relationship:

3. Worthwhile : Fruitful :: Futile : ________?

   Worthwhile : Fruitful :: Futile : **Useless**

   Relationship:

4. Mechanic : Automobiles :: Veterinarian : ________?

   Mechanic : Automobiles :: Veterinarian : **Animals**

   Relationship:

5. Biased : Prejudiced :: Balanced : ________?

   Biased : Prejudiced :: Balanced : **Fair**

   Relationship:

C. Do it all:

6. Teacher : Class :: Maestro : ________?

   Relationship:

7. Year : Decade :: One : ________?

   Relationship:

8. Convex : Concave :: Horizontal : ________?

   Relationship:

9. Nation : President :: State : ________?

   Relationship:

10. Enter : Exit :: Import : _________?

Relationship:

11. Cancer : Disease :: Biography : _________?

Relationship:

12. Gills : Fish :: Nose : _________?

Relationship:

Think About Analogy Thinking!

What **thought processes** do you call upon to solve these problems?

Write down at least three Tools you use.

13. Revolution : Government :: Mutiny : ________?

Relationship:

14. Angle : Triangle :: Chapter : ________?

Relationship:

15. Paradox : Puzzle :: Mirage : ________?

Relationship:

16. Radius : Diameter :: $\frac{1}{2}$: ________?

Relationship:

17. Humid : Moist :: Arid : _________?

    Relationship:

18. Enemy : Ally :: Opponent : _________?

    Relationship:

19. Cumbersome : Clumsy :: Poise : __________?

    Relationship:

These analogy problems above are pale imitations of the power of using analogies as a method of aiding thought. Instructors, textbook writers and professionals use analogies to explain complicated terms, concepts, or processes. They use them to make comparisons between two things, one of which may be familiar and another one unfamiliar or very complicated. Why do they do this? Because the only way any of us learn new things is by relating them to things we already know.

If we understand a familiar relationship, that helps us understand an unfamiliar relationship. Students learn to better understand electrical wiring or the body's circulatory system by relating either of them to plumbing. Have you ever tried to describe a new taste by relating it to something else, or a person you have just met by comparing him or her to someone else? When you do that you are using analogies and patterns.

You also use analogies when you try to remember what a word means. When trying to remember the difference between lines of longitude and latitude it helps to think of lines of **lat**itude as being similar to the rungs of a **lad**der. The first syllable of latitude is **lat** and the first syllable of ladder is **lad.** The sounds are similar. Tying unfamiliar knowledge to familiar knowledge provides a helpful thinking tool in the form of memory cues.

For a final activity, you create two analogies. Below, write all four words of the analogy, and then explain the relationship. Share your analogies with others and see how they rate your ability to create analogies.

20. Analogy 1:

    Relationship:

21. Analogy 2:

    Relationship:

Exercise 3d

One Day In The Life Of Jim Sweat

Here is Jim Sweat — a student, husband, father, and worker. He is not like most college students, but he is like some of them. As you read about one day in his life, look for patterns.

A few minutes after 7 a.m., Jim's wife, who has just come home from the hospital on third shift as a nurse's aide, wakes him up. He growls, "It can't be time to get up!" and rolls over for another 20 minutes of sleep. She goes into the kitchen to fix breakfast. He knows she will come back to check on him after she gets their 5-year-old son up, and Jim will still have time to make it to school.

When Jim finally stumbles out of bed, his son is crying because he does not have Lucky Struck cereal. Jim roars, "Cut that wailing out — you ought to be glad to get fed! Eggs are better for you anyway!" The boy sniffles and eats toast.

Things are quiet at the breakfast table until his wife hesitantly says that the used car he bought her was scratched in the parking lot while she was working. He says, "If you are going to let that happen to a nice car, you'd better ride to work with Martha across the street! I need the car anyway."

Just after that Jim gets up, says "Love ya," to his wife and son, and drives to school.

Jim's first class concerns electronics theory, and he has not read the assignment. He tries to bluff his way through a class discussion, but he can tell the instructor is not impressed.

He decides not to go to his afternoon classes because he has not studied or done his homework. The classes are boring anyway. Jim does not feel like studying for tomorrow's tests either. He thinks about going home but decides that his wife will probably have a friend over or be sleeping. It is a long trip, anyway.

Jim is pleased when Juan asks him to have a beer before they go to work second shift at the plant. They are both getting part of their tuition paid by the company and both are hoping for a promotion.

Jim is afraid that Juan has already been offered the job he wants for himself. He would really like to talk about it but just cannot bring it up. They do talk about how important it is to be a good father and husband, and agree that Jim is pretty rotten to pay so little attention to his family.

They also discuss going to school and agree that it is a drag sometimes. But they both believe that college might lead to a promotion because they will learn so much. Juan and Jim both seem to agree that although they know more about work procedures than some of the people who supervise them, it is the degree that matters to the company.

They spend a long time talking about the pressure of working, going to school, and keeping a wife and family happy. They agree that there never seems to be any time to do what they want to do.

Later, the talk moves to a recent incident at the Unionville Pirate's baseball game. A new manager has been showing a lot of promise for the team but really blew his cool and cursed the umpire and another team's manager publicly. Jim tells Juan that the manager had better shape up because he will never be able to use his talent if he cannot keep his temper.

At work, Jim is tired and really not in the mood to work. He wonders if he should have checked with his wife before he went to work but decides that it does not matter. One of his co-workers tells him he is grumpy and kids him some. Jim screams at the man and would have hit him if his supervisor had not stopped him. Finally the shift is over.

Jim stops by his mother-in-law's house to pick up his son, since by now his wife has gone to work. The mother-in-law tells Jim that the boy wet the bed again and really needs more attention. Jim agrees just to get his mother-in-law off his back. He nestles the sleeping boy down in the seat with his teddy and drives home.

At home his son wakes up and chatters about the frog he found at Gramma's house. Jim puts him to bed without finding out what happened at Gramma's. He picks up his electronics book, reads a page or two, but cannot concentrate on it. He turns on the TV for a show, drinks a couple of beers, and goes to bed.

1. What patterns do you find in what Jim **says**?

2. What patterns do you find in what Jim **does and does not do**?

3. How do the patterns of Jim's actions match the patterns of his words?

4. Predict Jim Sweat's future. List at least four things that you think will be true or might happen to Jim during the next three years, and explain why you think that might happen.
   a.

   b.

   c.

   d.

5. Finally, list one area of your own life where the pattern of what you say often does not match the pattern of what you do.

Exercise 3e

What Are Your Patterns?

We are surrounded by patterns. We live, love, act, judge, and think by the patterns we see. They make life predictable instead of just a series of random events.

All of us have our own patterns. We use them to do most things by habit, without having to think every tiny thing through. Other people use our patterns to judge, predict and identify us. When you are very late do your friends worry? If your pattern is always to be late they expect it. If your pattern is always to be on time they might worry and start looking for you.

Try to identify some of your patterns in three areas: school, personal situations and work.

1. List at least four of your **school patterns** (For example, on what kinds of tests do you do well?).

   a.

   b.

   c.

   d.

Why do your **academic** patterns matter? Give two reasons.

2. List at least four of your **personal patterns**:

   a.

   b.

   c.

   d.

   Why do your **personal** patterns matter? Give two reasons.

3. Give at least four of your **work patterns** (if you have not had paying jobs, think about home chores, etc.).

   a.

   b.

   c.

   d.

   Why do your **work patterns** matter? Give two reasons.

Exercise 3f

Using Thinking Tools With Patterns

You studied Thinking Tools in the last chapter. They will be a central part of each chapter. In this chapter we focus on how Thinking Tools function in recognizing and using patterns. You already use Thinking Tools for patterns; the goal is to become **aware** that you are using them and how you can use them.

First, look back at the exercises you have just done. What were you thinking? When you tackled those problems, what did your mind do and how was it doing it? Below, list three of those Tools that you think were especially useful in solving those pattern problems.

Now we will learn about our mental processes in another way. Following is another problem. Do not worry about finding the answer to the problem. Try to focus on your **mental activities** when you look for patterns. What are you comparing? What alternatives or information are you seeking? How do you know that is the right information? How are you trying to decide what is certain? **Think** about your thinking!

Elena and Sarah always eat lunch together. Here is what they ate this week:

Monday:	Elena	hamburger, fries, coke
	Sarah	salad, soup, milk
Tuesday:	Elena	spaghetti, corn, tea
	Sarah	cottage cheese, tea
Wednesday:	Elena	cheeseburger, pie, coke
	Sarah	salad, apple, coffee
Thursday:	Elena	grilled cheese, pie, coke
	Sarah	tuna salad, water
Friday:	Elena	hamburger, pie, milkshake
	Sarah	soup, tomato, tea

What pattern do you find in their lunches?

Think About It!

List **at least two new** tools that you did not list above.

Share your insights into your thinking processes with others in the class. Try to probe deeply into your thinking. Ask each other tough questions about what mental activity was occurring while you worked on this problem. List the resulting insights and ideas here.

Finally, solve the problem about Elena and Sarah. What pattern did you find?

In this book you go through the process of creating your own mental toolkit of Thinking Tools. In each chapter you will think seriously and carefully about the tools you want to add to the toolkit, based on what you did, thought and discovered in that chapter. In the box below list at least five Thinking Tools that are particularly important with pattern problems, and explain **how** they are useful.

My **Thinking Toolkit** Contains the Following Tools for **Patterns**:

Tool:

Use:

Tool:

Use:

Tool:

Use:

Tool:

Use:

Tool:

Use:

Supplemental Exercise 3g

Patterns In The Real World

Following are some situations and questions involving patterns. These situations underscore the importance of patterns in helping us make sense out of our lives.

1. Ann and Ari went to high school together and are going to the same college. They are both studying Radiologic Technology. They both took the same five courses in their first quarter but got very different grades. This confused them because they always got about the same grades in high school. They are trying to figure out what happened. Here are their scores. See if you can help them find the pattern.

Ari	Course	Ann
A	English	C
C	Mathematics	A
C	Chemistry	A
B	Radiologic Technology	B
A	Human Relations	C

Do you see any patterns? ___ Yes ___ No

If so, what are the patterns?

As they discussed it, Ari and Ann realized that each professor used a particular type of test consistently. Some only asked questions about the "big picture," with essay questions, applications and so on. Some always used questions about the details, with multiple choice, true-false and similar tests. Only a few instructors used both kinds of questions.

Ann and Ari also discovered to their surprise that they had developed different study habits in high school. One of them memorized details. The other looked for broad patterns and implications. The first did best on "detail" tests and the second did best on "big picture" tests.

Given the information that English and Human Relations were courses in which the instructor tested for the "big picture," and given Ann's and Ari's final grades, you should be able to answer these questions about their patterns.

a. Ari's study pattern is:

b. Ann's study pattern is:

c. The course that mixes memorization and the "big picture" is:

d. If Ari and Ann enroll in courses where the tests do not match their study patterns, what should they do?

e. Think about your own test preferences. Are you more like Ann or like Ari?

What implications do these insights have for you as a college student?

2. Alice's father is an old-fashioned farmer. He says that weather will just be good or bad, and there is no way to predict it. Alice does not believe that. She thinks you can figure out weather patterns. She studies the farm records for the past eleven years. She looks for four situations: lots of rain, especially hot, especially windy and drought. Here is what she finds out about the weather conditions each year:

Year	**Unusual Weather Conditions**
1	Rainy and hot
2	Windy and dry
3	Rainy
4	Hot and windy
5	Dry and rainy (!)
6	Windy
7	Rainy and hot
8	Windy and dry
9	?
10	?
11	?

Did Alice find any patterns in the first eight years? She did. Let's see if we can find them too.

a. What is the pattern for the years in which it is particularly rainy? *Hint: Underline **rainy** on the chart above.*

b. What is the pattern for years in which it is particularly dry?

c. What are the patterns for other unusual kinds of weather? List them here.

Can you put Alice's patterns together? See if you can predict the unusual weather Alice found for years 9 through 11.

d. What unusual weather did she find for year 9?

e. What unusual weather occurred in year 10?

f. What unusual weather occurred in year 11?

Alice is a smart person. She finds out which crops do badly in various situations. Here is what she discovers:

Wheat	does badly in either	Heat or Rain
Corn	does badly in either	Rain or Drought
Beans	do badly in either	Wind or Heat

g. Based on this information and the patterns you have discovered, when should Alice's father plant which crop? List the crops he should plant each year.

Hint: First figure out what unusual weather will occur each year.

Year	Plant Which Crop(s)?
12	
13	
14	
15	
16	

h. If Alice wants her father to spend a year on vacation from farming, which year should it be, based on these patterns?

3. Charlie was always a good student in high school, but he is having some trouble in college. He says he knows the material, but in some courses his test grades do not show it. He and his advisor go over his grades in English and business. Remembering Ari and Ann, they look at the types of tests given in these courses. Here is their data: the courses, the types of tests and Charlie's grades:

Course	Test Type	Grade
Literature	Essay	A
Accounting I	Multiple Choice	D
Composition I	Multiple Choice	B
Accounting II	Essay	C
Management	Multiple Choice	D
Composition II	Essay	A
Supervision	Essay	C
Grammar	Multiple Choice	B

a. How many patterns can you find?

b. What are the patterns in the kinds of tests?

c. What are the patterns in the types of courses?

d. What grades do you predict Charlie will receive in the following courses, based on these patterns? Write in the grades you think he will get, and your reasons.

- Business management (essay tests)

  Reason:

- Report writing (multiple choice)

  Reason:

- American poetry (essay tests)

  Reason:

- Business organization (multiple choice)

  Reason:

e. What should Charlie do once he recognizes these patterns? List three actions he could take.

Discuss this question with others in the class.

Supplemental Exercise 3h

More Thinking About Number And Letter Patterns

An earlier exercise in this chapter concentrated on ways of deciphering the patterns in number and letter sequences. In that exercise you created a system for solving those problems. Write that system in the space below.

Below are some additional pattern problems. Apply your system to these problems and figure out both the patterns and the final answers to each one.

1. 70, 71, 69, 70, 68, 69, ___, ___, ___, ___

2. 6, 8, 11, 15, 20, ___, ___, ___, ___

3. 6, 12, 14, 7, 14, 16, ___, ___, ___, ___

4. 4, 7, 6, 12, 15, 14, ___, ___, ___, ___

5. 0, 5, 50, 10, 15, 150, ___, ___, ___, ___

6. 20, 18, 15, 25, 23, 20, 30, ___, ___, ___, ___

7. 10, 5, 20, 10, 40, 20, ___, ___, ___, ___

8. 0, 3, 4, 4, 7, 8, 8, ___, ___, ___, ___

9. G, D, E, J, G, H, ___, ___, ___, ___

10. B, D, B, D, H, F, ___, ___, ___, ___

Did your system work for the letter problems? If it did not work completely, decide how to improve it and write the improved version here.

List at least three Thinking Tools that you are aware of using with these pattern problems.

Supplemental Exercise 3i

Final Thinking About Analogy Problems

The analogy exercise earlier in this chapter described a procedure for solving this type of problem, based upon the fact that a standard analogy in a test situation is based on two pairs of words. Below, write out the basic method of solving those analogy problems. Feel free to use the earlier exercise as a resource.

With that system in mind, solve the following analogy problems. Also explain the basic relationship within each pair.

1. Ham : Eggs :: Hamburgers : _______________?

   a. French Fries
   b. Jelly
   c. Leather
   d. McDonalds

   Relationship:

2. Collision : Confusion :: Infection : _______________?

   a. Pain
   b. Doctors
   c. Music
   d. Iodine

   Relationship:

3. Frog : Pond :: Bird : _______________?

   a. Egg
   b. Lilies
   c. Moon
   d. Sky

   Relationship:

4. Student : Class :: Cow : _______________?

   a. Herd
   b. Calf
   c. Cowboy
   d. Hamburger

   Relationship:

5. Free Man : Slave :: Private : _______________?

   a. Soldier
   b. Senator
   c. General
   d. Hero

   Relationship:

6. Medal : Brave :: Degree : _______________?

   a. Test
   b. Education
   c. Thermometer
   d. Third

   Relationship:

7. Panic : Earthquake :: Suicide : _______________?

   a. Anger
   b. Fear
   c. Pistol
   d. Depression

   Relationship:

8. Pencil : Paper :: Biscuit : _______________?

   a. Bank
   b. Catalog
   c. Stranger
   d. History

   Relationship:

Did your system for solving analogy problems work well? If not, write a revised version here.

Finally, list below at least three Thinking Tools that you found yourself using when you tried to solve the eighth problem above.

Chapter Four

Cause - and - Effect Thinking

Learning — academic and vocational — is a muddle of cause-and-effect relationships, to be approached thoughtfully.

This chapter is about **causes and effects** — one thing happens because another thing happens first. The hammer hits the nail (cause) and the nail goes into the wood (effect). The engine quits (cause) and the plane crashes (effect). The second thing happens because of the first thing.

You will improve six skills in this chapter. You will be able to:

- ❑ identify whether or not something happened because of something else.
- ❑ think of possible causes of certain events.
- ❑ identify the possible results of certain actions.
- ❑ identify mistakes in cause-and-effect thinking.
- ❑ recognize cause-and-effect relationships in written material.
- ❑ identify some Thinking Tools that are useful in cause-and-effect situations.

In solving problems and thinking you can use cause-and-effect skills at least three important ways:

You can predict possible outcomes from a given action. You can think ahead. You can figure out what might happen if you do something or do not do something. If you join a sports team you can predict that you will meet new people and get some exercise. If you do not join the team, you can predict that you will keep your time free for other things.

You can identify possible causes for a given event. You can make a good guess as to why something happened or did not happen. If the car does not start, you can guess that it might be out of gas or have a dead battery. With that guess in mind, you can then try to discover the actual problem and fix it.

You can figure out what you can do to make something happen. You can decide what result you want and then figure out how to cause it. If you want to graduate from college you can figure out what to do. Studying, giving up some other commitments, and attending classes regularly are some probable causes for the effect of college graduation.

Sometimes it is easy to get confused about cause-and-effect, and this can lead you into the following common mistakes:

Thinking that two things must be related. Two things happening at about the same time are not necessarily related. Imagine you sleep with your book under your pillow and then pass a test. That does not mean that the two are related. Sleeping with the book under your pillow did not cause you to pass the test. Much research identifies ways in which people do learn, but no research has ever pinpointed the pillow technique as effective. It was only coincidence.

Reversing cause-and-effect relationships. Sometimes we get mixed up and try to fix the wrong part of the relationship. For example, we might say: "That factory has lazy workers and screaming supervisors. So let's get rid of the screaming supervisors, and there will be no more lazy workers." This conclusion may confuse the actual cause (lazy workers) with the effect (what makes supervisors scream).

Sometimes we are not sure about cause-and-effect relationships. There are some words and phrases that help us. Words and phrases like "therefore," "because" and "as a result" indicate we are dealing with a cause-and-effect situation. That in turn helps us make decisions.

Exercise 4a

Thinking About Cause-and-Effect Versus Coincidence

Below are listed pairs of items. Some have cause-and-effect relationships; others simply suggest coincidences. Your task in this exercise is to decipher cause-and-effect relationships. Draw a right-facing arrow (like the first example) if the first part causes the second part. Draw a left-facing arrow (like the second example) if the second part causes the first part. Draw no arrow (like the third example) if no cause-and-effect relationship exists between the two items. Put a ✔ before each pair that has a cause-and-effect relationship.

✔ 1. Smoking. Lung cancer.

Smoking. → *Lung cancer.*

✔ 2. Smaller babies. Pregnant mothers who smoke.

Smaller babies. ← *Pregnant mothers who smoke.*

___ 3. Buying fire insurance. Protection from fire.

No cause-and-effect relationship.

___ 4. Eating rich food late at night. Restless sleep.

___ 5. A college degree. Success.

___ 6. Drinking diet sodas. Skinny body.

___ 7. Lack of rest and a poor diet. Less body resistance to illness.

___	8. Hard work.	Reward.
___	9. Buying a home computer.	Job promotion.
___	10. Chronic illness.	Heavy absenteeism.
___	11. Heavy traffic.	Auto accidents.
___	12. Red hair.	Hot temper.
___	13. Classes start at 8:15.	Many of the students seem to arrive at 8:10.
___	14. My friend is mad at me.	I am depressed.
___	15. Brushing with Crust toothpaste.	Popularity.
___	16. Buying life insurance.	Living longer.
___	17. Acne.	Eating chocolate.
___	18. Damaged hearing.	Listening to loud rock music.

Now share your answers with your team or with the whole class. Discuss the differences among your answers.

Discuss this question: How do you decide if a situation represents a cause-and-effect relationship or is simply a coincidence?

Exercise 4b

Thinking About Cause-and-Effect Chains And Clues

Many of the explanations, excuses and stories which others tell us are based on cause-and-effect relationships. Often we understand such tales only because we can understand the cause-and-effect words that glue the parts together. In this exercise we will look at two parts of this phenomenon: the chains of relationships that people can build and the clue words we use to understand cause-and-effect relationships.

1. Below is what is called a **cause-and-effect chain** — a series of statements that state or imply that each event is caused by the one before it. Read the statements and then answer the questions that follow them.

   - George wanted to be at school early for registration — it was his first quarter at the Mallory Community College.
   - He overslept because his alarm did not go off.
   - Therefore he started out 30 minutes late.
   - So he drove very fast to make up for lost time.
   - As a result a policeman stopped him and gave him a ticket — that took another 15 minutes.
   - Consequently he got to school after registration started.
   - Therefore he had to park so far from the auditorium that it took him another 15 minutes to walk there.
   - Thus even though he rushed he had to wait at the end of a long line to see his advisor about his business courses.

- Because he was rushing he did not notice that he was supposed to get his admission papers at the front door.
- So when he finally got to his advisor, the advisor told him to get his admissions papers first.
- Therefore George had to go back and get in another long line.
- He then had to wait another 45 minutes to get the papers.
- Therefore by the time he got his papers his advisor had gone to lunch and would not return until 1:15.
- As a consequence George realized that since he had to be at work as a truck driver at 2:30 he could not possibly complete registration that day.
- Because he could not complete registration, George decided not to attend college at all that quarter.
- So he worked a great deal of overtime since he had nothing else to do.
- But all the overtime made him very tired.
- And as a result of his tiredness George had an accident and broke his neck.

Now here are some questions about this **cause-and-effect chain.**

a. Did the policeman cause George to break his neck by making him later for registration than he would otherwise have been? Why or why not?

b. Did the alarm clock cause George to break his neck by making him start out late? Why or why not?

c. Did the advisor cause George to break his neck by going to lunch when George wanted to register? Why or why not?

d. What did cause George to break his neck? Why?

e. What contributed to George's breaking his neck?

f. Share your answers with others and see what they think. Then change your answers above if you wish.

g. What does this tell you about cause-and-effect thinking?

2. Do you remember someone telling you a long story about something that happened to him or her and emphasizing how one person did this, which led to that, which caused the other? Eventually the person concluded that the nasty thing which happened (or the nasty thing she or he did) was someone else's fault. That is very similar to blaming the policeman for George's accident.

   This person was giving you a cause-and-effect chain. Perhaps the only way you were able to follow what was being said was by finding cause-and-effect clues among the flow of words. This is natural. Our entire flow of explanations and reasons is built of cause-and-effect and so you sort out clues to those relationships without even being aware of it. It is now time to become aware of the cause-and-effect clues you find all around you.

   a. Look back over George's saga and underline all of the key words you can find in that sequence of events.

   b. Share the words you underlined with others in the class and explain any words you underlined which they did not.

   c. Now think about textbooks. The ability to spot cause-and-effect relationships can be a major aid in reading. As you read your college textbooks be alert for key words which signal a cause-and-effect relationship among ideas or facts. How will spotting those relationships increase your understanding of the textbook's content? Answer that question in the space below.

d. Below, list as many key words and phrases as you can think of which suggest cause-and-effect situations. Two examples are given.

- Because of …
- Reasons why …
-
-
-
-
-
-
-
-
-

e. Share your answers with others, add words or phrases which they suggest, and then put a star beside those words or phrases which you think **always** signal cause-and-effect thinking.

Exercise 4c

Thinking About Student Effects On The Instructor

The instructor's behavior has a definite effect on you as a student. A sharp-tongued, intolerant instructor might cause you to be quieter or more tense in class. A fast-paced, well-organized instructor might cause you to be more alert and mentally active. A sensitive, personal instructor might cause you to be more relaxed and willing to participate in class.

You also have an effect on the instructor. What you do and say, or do not do and say, influences how the instructor acts, feels and thinks. An instructor can make the difference between a good and a poor course. The students can make the same difference.

Below are listed some student actions. For each one identify a possible effect that the action might have on the instructor (how the instructor would feel, think or act towards you). The first is completed as an example.

1. You sit at the front of the class.

   The instructor mentally classifies you as a student interested in learning.

2. You forget to bring your book to class.

3. You spend the class period whispering to a friend.

4. You try to answer every question that the instructor asks the class.

5. You sit at the back of the class.

6. You miss two class periods in a row.

7. You have your notebook out and ready by the time the class starts.

8. You go to the instructor's office to ask questions about an assignment.

9. You look at your grade on your first test but do not look to see which questions you missed.

10. You are careful to write all of your homework and assignments neatly.

11. You regularly arrive at class a few minutes late.

12. You draw in your notebook during class.

Imagine that an effect you want is this: *to have the instructor think positively about me as a student.*

- Which of the actions listed above would you take as ways to cause that effect to occur? List their numbers below.

- Which of these actions do you often do?

- List at least three other actions you could take which might help cause that effect to occur.

What **Thinking Tools** Are You Using?

Exercise 4d

Cause-and-Effect, ... Or Not?

Below are some quotes. Your job is to decide which ones are cause-and-effect statements and which ones are not. Put an "X" before the ones that are not good examples of cause-and-effect relationships.. Then make brief notes on why they are not and on the Thinking Tools you used in deciding.

1. "Our sales force has been much more productive since we started hiring only women and paying them only for what they sold. That just goes to show that women make better workers!"

2. "Bob stayed out on the beach all day yesterday to celebrate the Fourth of July. That's why he's sunburned today."

3. "Jan studies a lot and Marie parties all the time. But Marie gets much better grades than Jan. I guess the way to get good grades is to party a lot."

____ 4. "Research shows that students stay in their classrooms more and study harder when policemen patrol the halls. I guess those policemen are pretty good teachers."

____ 5. "Enrico made all A's the first two quarters! He must really play up to the instructors!"

____ 6. "Al is working on a degree in management at night. He must have heard that there will be some supervisors' jobs coming available at the plant."

____ 7. "Ali is never late for work and never absent. He must have heard that there will be some supervisors' jobs coming available at the plant."

____ 8. "I'm better qualified than Charlie, but he got the job. Probably those dummies were snowed by the fact that he was all dressed up for the interview, while I just went like I was — the real me, straight off the production line!"

____ 9. "Tom's changing to general business from computer programming. I'm sure it's because he can't stand the pressure!"

____ 10. "For the last four years, studies have shown that the number of pigs slaughtered in Kansas has been almost exactly the same as the number of robberies in New York City. If they want to stop crime in New York City they just ought to stop raising pigs in Kansas!"

____ 11. "We put twice as many policemen on the street last year and crime was cut by 36 percent. We'd better keep them on the street if we want crime to stay down."

____ 12. "Turkish peasants say that the United States causes bad weather because they had terrible weather for the first three years after we landed a man on the moon. I wonder if they're right."

____ 13. "Tom's over 6' 6", weighs about 170 pounds and is always getting into fights. I guess he starts a lot of fights because he's so tall."

____ 14. "Dr. Brewer's always nasty to his students. No wonder his car was stolen!"

____ 15. "Spring is the rainy season. That's probably why all the flowers start blooming then."

____ 16. "Elliott takes a lot of notes in class and he really gets good grades! I guess taking notes helps you get good grades."

____ 17. "That kid is always grumpy when I pick her up from the sitter at 5:00. She must not like me."

Now it is your turn. Below, write two statements which sound like good cause and effect but which are really poor reasoning.

18.

19.

Think About Cause-and-Effect

What Thinking Tools enable you to recognize **cause-and-effect relationships?**

Exercise 4e

Needed: More Information

People almost never have enough information to make important decisions. They have to guess, predict or get more information. Here are some situations. In most of them there may be an important cause-and-effect relationship, but you are not sure. You may need more information.

1. Myrtle is very good at her secretarial job and is quite attractive. She is well trained and has a college degree. She knows more about the company than most of the other secretaries. She often volunteers to make presentations and head committees.

   Myrtle, however, feels the other secretaries have begun to shun her. They often stop talking when she enters the lounge, and they rarely invite her to go to lunch with them. It is obvious to the manager, Ms. Diem, that the other secretaries do not care for Myrtle.

   Myrtle has decided that they are jealous of her. She thinks that they have "little" minds because they cannot accept the fact that she is smarter and better looking than they are. It is their problem and not hers, she feels.

   a. What does Myrtle think is causing the other secretaries to act unfriendly toward her?

b. If Myrtle is right, what is she going to do about it?

c. Do you think Myrtle could be wrong? Explain your answer.

d. If Myrtle is wrong, what might be other causes of the secretaries acting unfriendly towards her?

e. What could Myrtle do to find out for sure?

2. Marcia, looking back over her 30 years, felt that she had been lucky to be in the right place at the right time. Finishing high school with honors, she got a scholarship to McQue University. While in college, she was selected to be the editor of the school newspaper. There she gained valuable experience in journalism.

   She was assigned to the public relations office as a work-study student and worked with the editors of all of the local newspapers. After graduating in the top 10 percent of her class, she was hired by one of the largest area newspapers as the society editor. Soon afterward she was promoted to feature editor. She won several state awards for features. Just this week she was hired by another newspaper as co-editor. Marcia considered herself very lucky to have been in the right place at the right time so often.

   a. What does Marcia think caused her success? Why?

   b. What do you think caused Marcia's success? Why?

3. Professor Higgins taught history in the fall semester by lecturing in class every day. He was distressed when 20 percent of the first semester freshman students failed the course. Professor Higgins decided to teach during the spring semester by assigning teams for discussion of topics, research papers and panel discussions. He did not lecture much. Only 5 percent of his second-semester freshmen failed his history course that time. Higgins decided that the change in his teaching techniques caused the students to do better.

   a. If Higgins is right and continues using these new techniques, should 95 percent of his students pass the course next fall?

   b. Why or why not?

   c. What other interpretations can we make of this situation?

   d. What can he do to be sure he has interpreted cause-and-effect correctly?

Exercise 4f

Using Thinking Tools For Cause-and-Effect

Cause-and-effect thinking is like fixing brakes on a car. It requires a variety of tools. In an earlier chapter you may have already listed a Thinking Tool something like this one:

Put yourself in the situation,
or
Imagine you are there,
or
Make the situation come alive.

Whatever you called it, it is a very useful tool with cause-and-effect relationships. To imagine the effects of an action, often you must put yourself in the place of another person and imagine how you would react in that situation. Imagining you are there is not always useful in solving a problem, but it frequently is a useful Thinking Tool with cause-and-effect situations.

Below, list three tools you have identified in earlier chapters which are also useful with cause-and-effect thinking. Describe carefully what your mind does with them in those situations. One example is listed.

1. One tool from earlier chapters that I also use with cause-and-effect is:

   Look for key words.

   And this is how I use it:

   When I see certain key words, this alerts me that there is a cause-and-effect relationship.

2. A second previously known Thinking Tool that I use with cause-and-effect statements is:

   And this is how I use it:

3. A third Thinking Tool that I use with cause-and-effect statements is:

   And this is how I use it:

4. A fourth Thinking Tool that I use with cause-and-effect statements is:

   And this is how I use it:

Now let's look at special Thinking Tools for cause-and-effect situations. Can you find at least two new Thinking Tools that you have used in this chapter, ones you did not list in the other chapters? At this point you may be a little overconfident. You may have identified several Thinking

Tools and have decided that they fit all situations. If so, you have just turned your brain off! There are many Thinking Tools which you use but still have not identified, and probably the best ones are still in your subconscious mind. In this chapter and each following one please strain to become aware of additional Thinking Tools which you use with particular types of problems. In this case, try to become aware of and list at least two new Thinking Tools and describe their use.

5. A new Thinking Tool that I discovered is:

   And this is how I use it:

6. Another new Thinking Tool that I discovered is:

   And this is how I use it:

Now for the hard part. You have listed six Thinking Tools above. They are very general skills, as you know. They are useful in many situations. A Thinking Tool is usually useful in jobs, personal lives and school. Can you determine how those five tools which you have identified are useful in three very common school situations: mathematics, reading and writing? Work with others to complete the following, being prepared to explain your answers.

7. The tools listed above that are useful with some kind of **mathematics** problems are:

8. The tools listed above that are useful in **reading** are:

9. The tools listed above that are useful in **writing** are:

Finally, complete the box below. List at least six especially important Thinking Tools that you would want in your mind when dealing with cause-and-effect problems. Revise and polish those six tools until they are as precise and powerful as you can make them.

My Thinking Toolkit Contains The Following Tools For **Cause-And-Effect** Problems

Supplemental Exercise 4g

Cause → Effect and Cause ← Effect

The title of this set of exercises is rather strange. Describe the title and write down what you think it might mean.

An important part of thinking is predicting what effects will be produced by a certain action or inaction. We do this continually when we think to ourselves ... "I wonder what will happen if I do or don't ... ." Fortunes, lives and nations are won or lost according to how accurately people predict possible effects.

The reverse situation is also true. We see a situation — an effect — and try to imagine the cause. If we see someone who is unusually depressed, or quits school, or has a big bandage on her head, what do we do? First we guess what caused the situation. If a businessman sees a competitor who is all smiles, what should he do? He had better figure out what pleases his competitor or he may find himself out of business!

It is very human to try to predict effects and figure out causes. That is what this exercise is about, and what the title of it means. The first half reads: "Cause → Effect." In other words, "This cause may lead to that effect." The arrow shows that we are moving from cause towards predicting possible effects. The other half reads: "Cause ← Effect," meaning that a certain outcome may have had a particular cause. Together they imply that, given either one, we can perhaps figure out the other.

Following are some situations. In each case, you know the cause or the effect, but not both. You must speculate on the missing half.

1. Helping A Friend Find A Job

There is a vacancy at the business where you work. Your supervisor asks you if you know of any one person you might want to recommend. You have three friends who are looking for a job. You can think of three actions that you might take but are trying to figure out what the outcomes might be. Below are listed the actions. In the first two cases one possible effect is listed. In all three cases think up and write down three possible outcomes of each action.

If	**Then**
I recommend all three,	a. *The boss might get mad.*
	b.
	c.
	d.

If	**Then**
I recommend none of them,	a. *They will get mad at me.*
	b.
	c.
	d.

If	**Then**
I recommend only one of them,	a.
	b.
	c.

2. Choosing Between School And Work

Betsy, a student at Markwell College, is trying to decide what to do about a work-study job that is open in the library. The advertised hours conflict with one of her courses. She needs the course, but she also needs the money. Betsy realizes that she cannot be in two places at once. She is thinking about what to do. Here are three choices she has considered. For each choice, complete the possible effects.

If	**Then**
She changes to another section of the course,	a. *She could have a harder instructor.*
	b.
	c.

If	**Then**
She drops the course,	a.
	b.
	c.

If	**Then**
She tries to switch the hours of the job,	a.
	b.
	c.

Think of at least one time in the last day that you have considered the consequences (effects) of a possible action. Share the situation and the effects you considered.

Supplemental Exercise 4h

Thinking About Influences On The Instructor Or Employer

Some students seem to think instructors are robots that live and breathe their subject matter. Perhaps instructors live in filing cabinets between courses! Actually, instructors do have lives beyond their school work and those lives have an effect on how they teach. Similarly, the lifestyle of the president of a company will affect how he runs his business.

Below are listed some facts about Mr. Nadir's life. See if you can figure out what effect they might have on his behavior as a chemistry teacher. Mr. Nadir:

- ❑ has three children, ages 20, 18, and 12;
- ❑ has a wife who works second shift in a textile plant;
- ❑ rides a bike 150 miles a week for exercise and fun;
- ❑ is trying to fix up a run-down house;
- ❑ takes care of the sick aunt who raised him;
- ❑ had a 15-year-old son killed in a robbery last year;
- ❑ quit a good job as an industrial chemist five years ago because he liked to help young people learn;
- ❑ now thinks that most students just want to get through college instead of learning things;
- ❑ is trying to save up for a new car by working a part-time job;
- ❑ feels like he never has any time to himself to learn more about chemistry or to think about where his life is going;
- ❑ reads history books as a hobby;
- ❑ and has had one mild heart attack and a continuing heart condition.

If all this is true, then what do you think Mr. Nadir might or might not do as an instructor?

His life will certainly affect his behavior as a teacher. List five major effects on his role as a teacher that you think his life situation might cause. One is given as an example.

1. *He might favor students who worked hard and seemed to want to learn chemistry.*

2.

3.

4.

5.

Circle the three effects above that you think are most likely to occur. Explain why they are the most probable effects.

I circled # ____ because:

I circled # ____ because:

I circled # ____ because:

Homework

Pick one of your instructors or employers and list at least eight facts about his or her background. If you do not know that many, figure out a way to find out. After you list them, write down at least three effects that you think these circumstances may have on her or him as a teacher/employer.

Supplemental Exercise 4i

Thinking About Who Is In Charge Of What

Dania is 20, lives at home, has always been very dependent. She lets other people and events determine her actions. She blames almost everything on others or on fate. Now she has decided to change that. She wants to become her own person, in charge of her life.

How does Dania do that? A counselor advised her to list the events that happened to her during a week. She can then look at them and see which ones helped her become more independent and which maintained her dependence.

Below are listed some of those events. Put an "I" before those that might help her be independent. Put a "D" before those that might keep her dependent. Put a "?" before any that do not affect it either way, but do not use "?" very often.

_____ 1. On Monday Dania bought two books she wanted to read and paid for them with some gas money.

_____ 2. She smoked two marijuana cigarettes one night.

_____ 3. Dania's car would not start Thursday morning so she did not try to get to school.

_____ 4. Her mother told Dania to watch her baby sister while doing her homework and she did.

_____ 5. She decided to study Tuesday night instead of going to a movie that her family wanted her to see.

_____ 6. Wednesday she went to her instructor after class to ask what she should study for the test.

_____ 7. Dania borrowed her friend's notes for the psychology course that she missed on Thursday.

_____ 8. She went out to eat because her friends wanted her to instead of going to Career Night at school.

_____ 9. Dania told her English teacher that she did not hand in a paper because she could not find a typewriter to use.

_____ 10. She applied for a part-time job at Hardees because she wanted more spending money.

_____ 11. She went to the math lab on Wednesday for help with some algebra problems she could not figure out.

_____ 12. She cut a test on Friday because it was to be an essay test and Dania had already decided she never did well on essay tests.

Discuss your answers with others. Defend the answers you put down. Explain why they are good conclusions for cause-and-effect relationships.

Now, also list five other things you think Dania could do to cause her to act more independently:

1.

2.

3.

4.

5.

How about you? We are all partly dependent and partly independent. Think over your own pattern of actions and decisions and answer these questions:

Are you mostly dependent or independent?

Why do you say that?

Think About It!

What are you thinking about as you try to solve these problems?

Write down the Thinking Tools you are using **now**.

Chapter Five

Testing Possibilities

We become better thinkers and learners when we look for more than one possibility or explanation — and test those hypotheses as best we can.

If we see a car coming toward us and swerving into our lane, what do we do? After we panic (if we do), we think about what choices we have — stop, bear right, bear left or swerve off the road. We try to figure out our possibilities.

An important result of improving our thinking skills is to become better at finding possible solutions. Another important result is that we get better at testing our possible solutions. In the case above we test the alternatives by imagining the consequences of each possible action — missing the car, going into a ditch, hitting a tree.

Many of us encounter a problem and immediately think we have the best solution. What we call further thinking is actually an attempt to prove that our solution is the best. It is our solution and we do not dare or care to look beyond it.

How do we make sure that this is the best choice? The most certain method in personal situations is to test all of the reasonable possibilities, which involves four stages. First, we think of all the reasonable alternative courses of action. Second, we try to be clear about our goal: the results we want (and the minimum we will accept) out of this situation. Third, we make a rough judgement of which alternative(s) seem most likely to achieve that result. Finally, we test all of those probable alternatives in order to determine the best choice.

These stages probably sound artificial when stated like this, but we do think this way. In an emergency we can move through all of these stages in only a few seconds. Like so many aspects of this book, these stages describe skills you already have and use. The intent is less to teach something new than to help you become conscious of and improve skills you already have. With that in mind, examine each of the four stages.

First, consider the number of possibilities open to you. The person who sees only one way to solve a problem may be narrow-minded, uncreative or simply lazy. There are often many ways a problem can be handled depending on the circumstances, the desired effect, the people involved. We become better thinkers when we learn to look for more than one possibility. The first stage is thus to brainstorm as many possibilities as you can even if some of them seem foolish at first.

Second, be clear about what you want. There is an old saying that "if you don't know where you are going, it is very hard to know when you have arrived." This very much applies to testing possibilities. You might identify several alternatives which at first glance seem good, but as soon as you state your goals clearly some of them seem much less attractive. You can only choose what is best for you when you have clarified what you want.

For instance, think about someone who is offered a bribe. He can take it, reject it or turn the person in to the police. Can he do more? He can hit the person, take the money and then turn the person in to the police. He has other alternatives. Which is best? It depends heavily on his being clear about what he wants in that situation. Does he want the money? Does he want to avoid embarrassment? Does he want the person jailed? Does he want to take out his tensions on the person? Any of the alternatives suggested above might be best for him depending on his goals.

Third, sort out all of the alternatives in light of your goals. You need to decide very generally which alternatives seem good and which do not. This is not your final decision. It simply identifies the most likely alternatives and therefore suggests where to start in your final stage of actually testing the possibilities.

By this point you have a general sense of how each alternative may or may not lead to your goal. You have an educated guess as to which alternative is best for you. This is called a hypothesis. A hypothesis is a tentative idea, argument or explanation. It is the most likely candidate for getting what you want and is therefore the first thing you should test.

How do you test your hypothesis? Gather and compare information. Imagine possible outcomes by putting yourself in the situation. Consider all of the relevant factors you can. Then decide how likely that hypothesis is to achieve what you want.

Fourth, treat the best two or three alternative hypotheses the same way, testing how well each one suits your need. See if any of them achieves more of your goal than your first hypothesis. When you finish this step, you will have tested all of your main hypotheses and can then choose thoughtfully. Your choice may still prove wrong, but if so it is not for lack of trying. You will have done all you can to find the preferred solution.

There is one final aspect of testing possibilities you must consider. The stages above describe how to test possibilities in terms of future actions — what you do now (turn left) in order to achieve your goal (miss the oncoming car). But we also constantly test possibilities concerning past and present events.

We hear about some important or interesting action and immediately start thinking about what caused it. We test many possible explanations for that past event. We may also notice a pattern of present behavior or action: someone always sitting alone in the cafeteria, or the freezing classrooms on Monday mornings in winter. What do we do? Again, we raise and test hypotheses about what causes that pattern.

The exact use of the four stages in testing possibilities may differ between past, present, and future possibilities. For example, our *goal* (stage two) when trying to explain someone's actions is to find that hypothesis which best fits all the known facts. That is not quite the same type of goal as when we assess future possibilities, but it plays the same role in the process. The stages in hypothesis testing, then, can be used to understand the past and present as well as partly to control the future.

Any of these uses can be a very long process. Scientists spent dozens of years testing possibilities before they created the atomic bomb: a test of hypotheses about the future. Juries can take months to reach a verdict: a test of hypotheses about the past. Often, however, it is a quick process. You do not have much time to test possibilities when a car is heading straight for your car! Your mind can work amazingly fast, and it does. It can test many possibilities in a few seconds.

This chapter will help you improve your ability to test possibilities. After completing it you will be able to:

- ❑ Formulate a hypothesis about how best to solve a problem.
- ❑ Judge hypotheses by looking at the evidence.
- ❑ Recognize the lack of evidence or proof for a given possibility.
- ❑ List other information that will help you test possibilities.
- ❑ List and explain Thinking Tools that you use in formulating and testing possibilities.

As a start on that process, answer the following questions. Do not just repeat the words used in this introduction. Answer in your own words.

1. What is the first stage in testing possibilities?

2. What is the second stage in testing possibilities?

3. What is the third stage in testing possibilities?

4. What is the final stage in testing possibilities?

5. Why is it important to improve your ability to consciously test possibilities?

6. What other things might you sometimes want to do when testing possibilities? See if you can list two more things.

7. What is the difference between *testing possibilities* and *cause-and-effect thinking?*

8. Discuss your answers with others in the class.

Exercise 5a

Testing Possibilities In Academic Situations

We naturally think through situations like those which follow when we encounter them in college. Walking through the process of testing possibilities in those situations will help you discover more about how your mind reacts to everyday choices or problems.

1. Ms. Murple, a 33-year-old faculty member at Pikesburg Technical College, has been a calm leader at the college. She is reliable, well respected by the administration, and seen by students as an excellent teacher who loves her work. You hear one day that she has quit without notice. It is natural to wonder why she left and to try to come up with a reasonable explanation. Your mental processes might resemble the cycle below of thinking of a possible explanation and then seeking evidence for or against it, then thinking of another possibility, and so forth.

   Hypothesis: "I wonder if she got fired?"

   Evidence: "I doubt it. Everyone liked and respected her."

   Hypothesis: "Maybe she's going to retire."

   Evidence: "Nope. She's too young, at 33."

   Hypothesis: "Perhaps she's taking leave to have a baby."

   Evidence: "I don't think so. She didn't look pregnant yesterday."

Hypothesis: "Could she have been caught in some crime?"

Evidence: "It doesn't seem likely. She's not the type."

Do you remember going through that kind of process in your mind in other situations? Describe an occasion when you thought through that type of situation.

Now it is your turn to think about Ms. Murple's departure.

a. Each pair above has a hypothesis and some evidence which tests it. Underline the evidence in each pair of statements.

b. Which of the pieces of evidence above seems weakest in proving or disproving the hypothesis? Put a checkmark before any pairs in which the evidence seems weak.

c. Can you find more evidence yourself? Fill in evidence for these hypotheses:

Hypothesis: "I wonder if she just didn't like teaching us?"

Evidence: "No, because:

Hypothesis: "Maybe it was just an impulse to go see the world."

Evidence: "Probably not, because:

d. Finally, identify two other hypotheses which might explain Ms. Murple's sudden decision. Write them below and find any evidence you can to support or deny those possibilities (there may not be any in the passage).

Hypothesis: Maybe she:

Evidence: because:

Hypothesis: Maybe she:

Evidence: because:

e. Share your answers with the class and discuss them.

2. Dr. Ramirez, Rico's electronics teacher, obviously loves electronics. He thinks it is an exciting thing to study. But he only gives one test and a final, and he says that it is up to the students whether or not they do the work in the course. He is impatient with students who do not learn quickly, although he will work long hours after class with those who want to learn electronics.

   Dr. Ramirez does not like "dumb" questions. Rico asks a lot of questions meant to impress the instructor, but sometimes Dr. Ramirez seems to think they are dumb questions. Rico has failed the course once. He hears another student comment that Dr. Ramirez does not seem to like Rico, and Rico is trying to figure out why that might be. Here is what he says to himself.

   - "Maybe he just doesn't like Chicanos."

     "That doesn't make sense, with a name like his!"

   - "Maybe he's upset because I told him yesterday that I'm only taking this course because it's required."

     "Probably, since he thinks electronics is so important and interesting."

   - "Since he doesn't seem to care if we study or do our work, he may not be mad at me just because I don't usually do my homework."

   a. Underline the hypothesis and the evidence used to test it in each of the pairs above.

b. Fill in possible evidence (if you can find any in the passage above) for the following three hypotheses:

- "Could he be mad because I don't treat him like a king? I tell him what I think."

- "Could he realize that I try to con him?"

- "Maybe he doesn't like me because I failed the course once."

c. Which of the pieces of evidence in *b* seem weakest to you in terms of proving the hypothesis? Put a checkmark before the pieces of evidence that seem weakest.

d. Identify two more possible explanations for this situation. List the kind of evidence you would try to find to prove or disprove those two hypotheses.

- Maybe:

  Evidence?

- Maybe:

  Evidence?

e. Share your responses with a team or the whole class. Defend your answers (and listen to their answers). Add any other answers or ideas that you hear which seem good.

f. List some things that Rico could do to improve Dr. Ramirez's opinion of him.

-
-
-
-

Exercise 5b

Hypothesis Testing — A Tool That Changes The World

Hypothesis testing sounds fancy and complicated. We hope you now realize that it is not — it is something we all do every day. It is important to know this and then test our hypotheses carefully.

Testing hypotheses changes our personal world. It also changes the larger world we live in for it is the key to western civilization. What has resulted from hypothesis testing? The nuclear bomb, drought-resistant corn, LSD, skyscrapers, peanut butter, the welfare system, Hardee's, paperback books and community colleges are only a few of the results. Do you believe that? Below are some examples of how hypothesis testing has changed the way we live.

Someone years ago looked at some weeds called peanuts and imagined many possibilities for what could be done with them. He raised many hypotheses. He then tested them by planting, changing the growing conditions, and processing peanuts in many ways (squeezing, rotting, puffing, and so on). The results? He proved many of his hypotheses and discovered over a hundred good uses for the peanut. His name? George Washington Carver.

Someone else recently examined people's travel, work and eating habits. He also examined patterns of restaurants, businesses and financing. He raised many hypotheses, all related to a central idea. He generated a hypothesis that Americans would patronize a new type of restaurant where the food and prices were identical across the country. His name? Ray Krock. His brainchild? McDonalds. Fast food restaurants are a way of life today, but began with some hypotheses.

A third American imagined different ways to manufacture things. He looked at the standard factories of his time and noticed that every worker made the whole machine or item. He generated many hypotheses about a different method of manufacturing, where each person did only a small part of the total job but repeated it many times. The items to be built would move on belts from one of these specialists to another. This person's name? Henry Ford. His product? Automobiles. His contribution? A new method of production called the assembly line. It became the basis for almost all of our modern industries.

Hypothesis testing is the key to much of our world. Beneath that, though, is our own willingness to raise hypotheses. We need to observe and be puzzled by what we see around us. We need to imagine possible explanations. Then we need to test our hypotheses — to figure out how to try them out, to gather evidence, and to see if our ideas fit the real world. We test, and then gradually we determine whether our ideas are right.

1. Below are listed some situations. Study them to see if the people involved have raised and tested their hypotheses with care.

    a. A man sees his girlfriend with another man, decides she is stepping out on him and leaves her.

    b. A man never notices that his girlfriend is seeing another man.

    c. Someone hears that a worker is lazy and always trying to do as little as possible. He then observes that worker's performance for six weeks before deciding that the rumor is accurate.

    d. Someone is advised by a college counselor to switch programs because "welding is not for her." She checks with the department head, observes other students, and reads descriptions of the program of study before deciding to stay in the welding program.

e. Someone hears that his state's first black sheriff in 92 years is arrested for bribery, reads a newspaper account of the event, and then decides that the sheriff is or is not guilty mainly because the sheriff is black.

f. A woman applies for a job, loses out to a man, and immediately files a lawsuit for discrimination.

g. A supervisor is aware that morale among the workers is low. He considers either raising the hourly wage or perhaps hiring more people, but then decides to send a survey around to all workers first.

h. A student enrolls in a math course and is told by a former student that the instructor is very hard, does not help the students, and allows few students to pass. Therefore the student drops the course on the second day.

i. A student has financial problems and thinks he may have to drop out of school because he cannot afford any more tuition. He makes an appointment with the financial aid advisor to find out if he is eligible for a grant or the work-study program.

2. Place a checkmark in front of each of those situations above which you think represent good hypothesis testing.

3. Discuss your decisions with others and give explanations.

4. Now answer this question: What is the difference between good and poor hypothesis testing?

5. Share your answers with the class and note any good points that they make.

Exercise 5c

Testing Possibilities In Personal And Professional Situations

The types of hypothesis-testing skills we employ in the college situations dealt with earlier are equally critical in our personal and professional lives. Here are two examples of such applications.

1. The Northside Tigers always play their last football game of the year against their traditional rivals, the Fulton Bearcats. You have moved away from the area but always keep up with the Tigers. You are concerned this year because Northside has a new coach and the Bearcats are undefeated. In the newspaper you read that the Bearcats won by a score of 21 to 10.

   The article notes that the Tigers had 55 yards in penalties while the Bearcats were penalized 45 yards. It also says that the Bearcats gained 327 yards compared to the Tigers' 174 yards. It quotes the Tigers' coach as saying before the game: "We're really up for this one, and we've never been in better physical shape!"

   Naturally, you wonder why the Tigers might have lost the game. Here are some things that might go through your head.

   - "Probably our first-string quarterback was sick."

     "Nope, because it says everyone was healthy."

   - "Maybe they got too excited and never settled down."

     "That might be it. The coach said they were really up for the game."

- "There doesn't seem to be any evidence in the story of a payoff or crooked deal."

  "The yards penalized were pretty much the same, so I don't think they got beat by their own mistakes."

You are naturally and repeatedly raising possibilities and testing them as these thoughts occur.

a. First, underline the evidence used to test the hypothesis in each of the four pairs listed previously.

b. Second, fill in your evidence (or lack of it) for the two possibilities below.

   1. "Could the Bearcats have simply been the better team?"

   2. "I wonder if that new coach did a bad job of coaching."

c. Which pieces of evidence seem weakest to you in terms of proving or disproving any of the above hypotheses? Put a checkmark before them.

d. What other possible explanations can you think of to explain the Tigers' loss? List at least two hypotheses and the kinds of evidence you would look for (not just evidence in the passage) to prove or disprove the hypotheses.

Maybe:

Evidence:

Maybe:

Evidence:

2. Your friend Erica is trying to buy a car. You are helping her. You see an ad in the newspaper for a Toyota at a very good price. It is being sold privately, not by a dealer. You go to see it, and the owner explains that he has to sell it because they have a new baby and need the money. You inspect the car and think that perhaps the side door is a slightly different shade than the rest of the car. The finish on that door is very smooth, and it apparently has no dents or nicks although the car as a whole looks a little scratched and dented.

   The car is one and one-half years old and light blue in color. The owner says that you could test drive it, but it has a flat tire (ran over a nail, he says). He seems very pleasant and is quite good looking. The odometer shows 23,278 miles. He says he will come down a little in price if you will buy it now, because he needs the money quickly for the rent.

a. Test each of the following hypotheses by listing after each item any evidence you can find for or against the possibility.

- "Maybe it's a stolen car."

- "Maybe it's been wrecked."

- "Maybe it's one of those once-in-a-lifetime good deals."

- "Maybe the odometer has been turned, and it has really gone over 123,000 miles."

- "Maybe he really will get kicked out of his apartment if we don't buy it now."

- "Maybe it's in mechanically bad condition."

b. Can you think of other possibilities in this situation? See if you can list at least two other hypotheses and also some evidence to test those possibilities.

- Maybe:

  Because:

- Maybe:

  Because:

c. List at least four pieces of evidence which are not given in the passage that you would like to have:

-
-
-
-

Think About It!

What are you thinking about as you try to solve these problems?

Write down what mental activities are occurring.

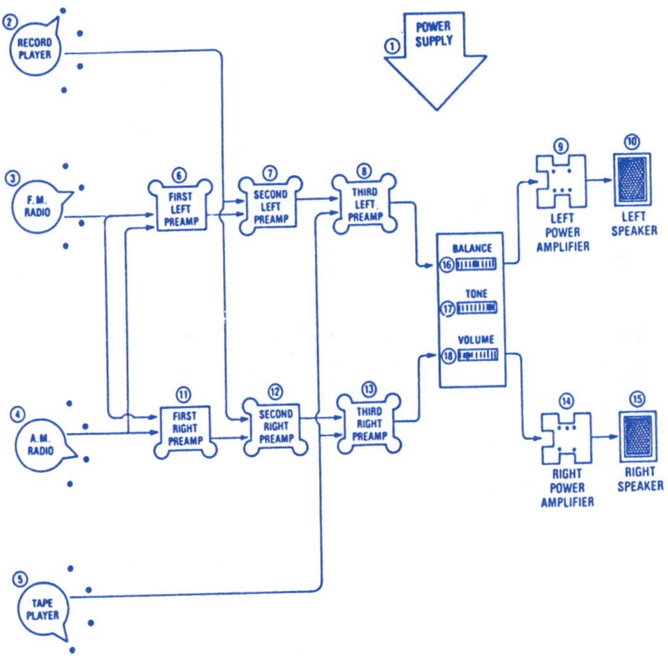

Stereo System

Exercise 5d

Troubleshooting A Stereo System

On the opposite page is a map of a stereo system. It includes some of the parts of the kind of stereo you probably have at home. Do not worry if it seems confusing at first. It is easy to understand if you study it for a few minutes.

The circular parts on the left side represent the switches of the stereo. The two sets of three items in the middle (with "left" or "right" on them) are amplifiers. The balance, tone and volume settings are towards the right, and the final two pairs of items on the right side of the page relate to the two speakers. All of the items are numbered as described below.

Part 1 — The power supply and plug (into the wall).

Parts 2-5 — Choice switches which turn the switch to the stereo function desired (tape player, AM radio, FM radio or record).

Parts 6-10 — The left channel (carries sound to the left speaker):

- Three devices (6-8) inside the stereo adjust the electrical signal in the left channel.
- The amplifier (9) automatically increases loudness.
- The left speaker (10)

Parts 11-15 The right channel (to the right speaker):

- Three devices (11-13) inside the stereo adjust the electrical signal in the right channel.
- An amplifier (14) automatically increases loudness.
- The right speaker (15)

Parts 16-18 The controls adjust the quality and location of the sound:

- Balance between right and left (16)
- Tone, low to high (17)
- Volume (18)

The lines between parts indicate the flow of electrical power. If a line does not go between two parts, then there is no electrical connection between them. For example, the Record Player setting controls electrical flow to the second left and right preamps (and beyond), but not to the first left and right preamps. The first pre-amps simply are not used and do not matter when the stereo is set for record player.

Usually you set the switches on the stereo the way you want, and if the parts work the stereo does what you want. If the stereo does not work, what do you (or the repairman) do? You generate and test hypotheses. You decide what is most likely to be the problem (or the easiest thing to check) and then test to determine if that is the problem. If that is the problem, you fix it if you can. If that is not the problem you find another hypothesis and test it.

1. Like many things, this may sound more confusing when explained in words than it actually is when you do it. You do this type of hypothesis testing often. Try these:

   a. You put a record on the stereo, turn on the power and hear the radio.

      - ❑ What is your hypothesis?

        I've forgotten to switch it to 'Record Player.'

      - ❑ How do you test it?

        See if the switch is on 'Record Player' and change it if it isn't.

   b. You put in a tape, turn on the stereo and hear only a faint sound.

      - ❑ What is your hypothesis?

      - ❑ How do you test it?

   c. You turn the stereo to your favorite FM radio station, turn it on and the sound only comes from the right speakers — but loud enough to send your younger sister screaming from the room.

      - ❑ What are your two hypotheses?

      - ❑ How do you test them?

All of these situations require *testing hypotheses*. They all involve the switches shown on the drawing (2-5 and 16-18), or some of the parts shown (such as 9). If your tests of the switches do not work, then the trouble probably relates to one or more of the other parts shown on the drawing (6-15). If you call a repair person, she or he will first doublecheck the switches (2-5, 16-18) on the outside. Then he or she will check the inside parts. What about part 1? Calling repair persons without checking the plug has cost stereo owners millions of dollars!

Now it is your turn to troubleshoot a few problems and generate a few hypotheses.

2. You turn on the stereo for FM radio. It works fine on the right speaker, but you hear nothing from the left speaker.

   a. What is the first thing you check?

   b. Why?

   c. How do you check it?

   d. If your first hypothesis does not work, what five other things could be wrong? List all of the parts (by number) that could go wrong and cause these symptoms.

      ❑ ❑

      ❑ ❑

      ❑

3. Now you want to turn on the AM radio for a snow alert to see if the schools will be closed. You turn on the power and the lights come on but you hear nothing.

   a. What three things do you check first?

   b. If these do not solve the problem, what are your remaining hypotheses about what could be wrong?

4. Now it is December. You want to play your favorite Christmas music while you are trimming the tree. You put on those tapes, turn on the power switch and nothing happens at all.

   a. What are your hypotheses? List all the possible things that could be wrong.

   b. Which ones could you, personally, check? Put a checkmark beside the ones above that you could check.

c. What are the first three parts you would check, in order?

5. You have just bought a new record by your favorite artist. You put it on and turn the power on. The left speaker is very, very soft and sounds squeaky. The right speaker is loud enough but very squeaky also.

    a. List all of the things that might be wrong: all of your hypotheses.

    b. Now list the things you think are most likely to be wrong.

6. Here is a final question about your stereo system. Assume that your AM radio gives no sound from the right speaker. This means that anything affecting the right channel can be the problem. What three things are the obvious choices for checking first? Why?

What Thinking Tool does that suggest to you?

Exercise 5e

Using Thinking Tools When Testing Possibilities

You use many Thinking Tools when testing possibilities. You try to understand the situation and the information you have. You try to imagine possible explanations. You look for evidence in what you read, hear or know. You sort through many thoughts at the same time.

Try to focus on your mind once again. Try now to explore how you actually use Thinking Tools when you generate and test hypotheses.

1. How does the Thinking Tool of *find and use key words* work when testing hypotheses? We use this tool in two special ways: to help us think of hypotheses and to help us test the hypotheses.

   Remember the problem about the car that Erica was thinking of buying? In the problem you noticed that the paint on one door was a slightly different color than the rest of the car. For a thoughtful car buyer that is a key observation. It triggers a possible hypothesis: the car has been wrecked and then repainted. The hypothesis is then tested by looking over the passage again for any other key words that could support the wrecked possibility. The Thinking Tool involving keys has thus been used in two ways.

   This is how key words help us think through hypotheses. Key words trigger possibilities. Other key words support or deny those possibilities.

- Turn back to Erica's problem in Exercise 5c and answer these two questions:

    a. What key words or phrases in the passage about Erica cause us to generate the hypothesis that the car might be in mechanically bad condition? Write those words or phrases here.

    b. With that hypothesis in mind, find other key words or phrases to support the hypothesis. Write them here.

Do you see how the mind uses key words to generate and test hypotheses? Try to be aware of this mental activity as you complete this chapter.

2. Try another exercise as a team. Following is a situation which you must deal with. Talk with each other about your thinking methods as you try to think through the situation. Be aware of your mind as it is working. Try to share your Thinking Tools with others on the team by talking actively about how you would deal with the situation.

You are walking along a street and discover an apparently dead man lying on the sidewalk. Your immediate question: "Why is he dead?"

a. How are you figuring out the possible explanations? What is your mind doing?

b. How are you deciding how to test those possibilities?

c. Share your answers and insights concerning the preceding question with the class and write down below what you learn from others about the Thinking Tools used to test possibilities.

d. By the way, what would you do if you discovered a dead person like that?

e. Why?

3. Here is one final situation. As you think it through, make a mental list of the Thinking Tools you are using.

> When you pick up your mail this afternoon you discover an envelope with no name on it containing $2,500 in cash.

After thinking this through, describe or list how your Thinking Tools helped you work your way through that situation.

1.

2.

3.

My Thinking Toolkit Contains
The Following Tools For
Testing Possibilities

Supplemental Exercise 5f

Testing Another Possibility

Thomas has applied for a sales job at McQuirter's, a local clothing store. The job only requires high school graduation, and he is graduating in two months from Questin Community College. He asked his department head this morning to write a letter of reference, and she said she would. He was called for an interview and went there directly from his job as a mechanic. He had to take time off from work to do it, but told the interviewers about this sacrifice to impress them with his interest. He made sure they understood what he had given up in order to interview with them.

Thomas was very surprised by some of the questions he was asked. Before he arrived, he had not thought much about answering questions. However, he tried to give the answers he thought they wanted. He had to "beef up" his experience, knowledge, and ideas a little bit, since his only real experience in selling was a six-month cooperative education assignment which required only three hours a week for a semester.

This afternoon Thomas heard that another student in his class got the job. He is angry, disappointed, wants to know why. List hypotheses for why Thomas did not get the job, and list some evidence from the passage above to support or deny those hypotheses.

Maybe:

Evidence:

Maybe:

Evidence:

Maybe:

Evidence:

Maybe:

Evidence:

Maybe:

Evidence:

Maybe:

Evidence:

What additional information does Thomas need to help him understand why he did not get the job? List that information here.

Discuss your answers with others in the class.

Chapter Six

Relevance In Thinking

Often, relevance is a matter of more or less instead of yes or no. It comes in all shapes and sizes, and only becomes valuable when thoughtfully used.

This chapter is about relevance. **Relevant** information relates to the situation at hand. It helps you understand something or solve a problem. If information is not relevant it is not helpful. Irrelevant information may confuse you, mislead you or just waste your time.

In this chapter, you will improve several thinking skills.
You will be better able to do these things:

- ❑ Judge how relevant information or arguments are to a situation.
- ❑ Identify the most relevant parts of a decision or problem.
- ❑ Identify arguments or information as irrelevant or only slightly relevant to a situation.
- ❑ Discover and polish Thinking Tools that you can use in many situations involving relevance.

Sometimes it is easy to decide what information is relevant. Let's say you are trying to decide whether or not to take a particular job. Is the job's salary relevant to your decision? Of course it is. Are the job's duties relevant? Yes. How about the supervisor's height? This is not usually relevant to your decision.

Often it is not easy to decide on relevance. Let's say you are considering a job and your supervisor would be a woman. Is that relevant? To some people the sex of the supervisor would be like the height — not relevant. But for other people it would be relevant. It might influence their decision.

Sometimes two pieces of information are relevant, but one is more relevant than the other. Look at an example. You are taking a final exam and get to class 10 minutes late. That is relevant since you have less time to finish the test. You also did not study at all, which is more relevant than your lateness. It will have more impact on your test grade.

Look at an example of how we judge the relevance of a piece of information according to our personal values, need or desires.

You are driving home from work or school, and you notice that your gas gauge is on "Empty." Your home is eight miles away from the last gas station. You are late and very tired. Should you stop for gas tonight or wait until the morning?

As is often true, the "right" answer is, "It depends." What does it depend on? Here are seven statements. Number them in order of what you think is the relevance of each piece of information with "1" being the information that most influences your decision, "2" being next most influential, etc.

____ A. The gas station may not be open in the morning.

____ B. Your gas gauge is not always accurate.

____ C. You're late for dinner.

____ D. You need a pack of cigarettes.

____ E. You have a splitting headache.

____ F. Maybe you can ride with a neighbor tomorrow.

____ G. You have to lead an important meeting early tomorrow.

You may have realized that all of these are relevant. The question is, how relevant? That depends on the situation and on your values, priorities and style.

If you are a highly task-oriented, conscientious or well-organized person, you might select G as the first priority (#1). The early morning presentation would greatly influence all other decisions. If, on the other hand, you believe in taking a risk, you might choose B as the first priority. A heavy smoker might choose D as most relevant.

A final item, which should be somewhat clear by this point, is that relevance depends on the use you plan to make of it. Nothing is ever relevant by itself — it is always relevant for something. Relevance thus means something different every time you deal with it. It is relevant only to a particular decision, problem, action or choice. When looking for relevance always ask, "relevant for what?"

Relevance, then, is a relative term rather than an absolute one. Information may be highly relevant to one person and one situation, less so to another and irrelevant to a third. Effective thinkers are usually skilled at isolating the things relevant to a particular situation.

Before you begin **relevance** exercises, identify some Thinking Tools that you predict will be helpful.

Exercise 6a

The Art Of Asking Relevant Questions

One of the most powerful uses of relevance is in asking questions. Questions are a vital way to get new, useful information. They can make the difference between a good decision or outcome and a poor one by making sure that you and others have a full, accurate picture before you decide or act. However, a question unasked is useless and asking an irrelevant question can hurt rather than help the situation. Asking relevant questions is an art; this exercise will help you investigate it.

1. In this situation, you are ready to buy a 5-year-old car from a dealer. Below are listed a series of questions that you might ask, some relevant and some not. Put a checkmark beside the 7-8 questions you think are most relevant in buying a 5-year-old car.

____ a. What is the car's top speed?

____ b. Has the car ever had a new battery?

____ c. Is that the car's original color?

____ d. Does the color match my hair?

____ e. What kind of mileage does the car get?

____ f. Does the car burn a lot of oil?

____ g. How many owners has the car had?

____ h. Does the car have snow tires?

____ i. Who owned the car before you got it?

____ j. How long does the warranty last?

____ k. What does the warranty cover?

____ l. Is it a standard or automatic shift?

____ m. What is the condition of the spare tire?

____ n. How many years have you been in business?

____ o. What is your reputation in the community?

____ p. What is the telephone number of the previous owner?

____ q. What does *Consumer Reports* say about that model of car?

____ r. Has the car been in any accidents?

____ s. How fast does the car accelerate 0-60?

____ t. What is the car's bluebook value?

Now share your answers with your team or the class. Decide as a group which ones you think are most relevant. You should circle the group's answers on the list to make sure you know which are like or different from your answers. Why is it important to identify relevant questions before you buy a car?

2. In this situation you are going for a job interview with a personnel officer. You know that job interviews are two-way streets. You will be asked questions, but you should also ask questions to discover relevant things about the job and the company. You are pondering a list of questions you might ask the personnel officer.

   Check the nine questions you think are most relevant and most wise to ask in an interview. If you do not like the way a question is phrased, change it. Be prepared to explain your answers.

   ____ a. What is the salary for this job?

   ____ b. What are the working hours?

   ____ c. Will I like the job?

   ____ d. What kind of insurance coverage do I get?

   ____ e. Can my sister have a job here, too?

   ____ f. This job does not require overtime, does it?

   ____ g. How long do I have to work here before I get sick days?

   ____ h. What are the working conditions like?

   ____ i. What job duties will I have?

   ____ j. What happens if I don't like my supervisor?

   ____ k. To where can I advance from this position?

   ____ l. If I leave, do I still get my vacation days?

   ____ m. Are you a unionized plant?

____ n. What are the educational requirements for the job?

____ o. If I get the job, how can I be sure you won't fire me?

____ p. Will I have to work the swing shift?

____ q. How much overtime can I expect to have?

____ r. If the kids get sick, can I take off work?

____ s. The job is not very noisy, is it?

Which answers did others rate as relevant that you did not? Write their letters down here.

Explain why their answers were different from yours.

Did you find any questions which were relevant, but which it was probably not wise to ask directly? If so, how can you handle that?

3. You are still preparing for your job interview. This time you are trying to figure out the questions she might ask you. Check the seven or eight questions that you think are relevant and fair from the employer's point of view.

____ a. What do you do on weekends?

____ b. Do you get sick a lot?

____ c. How much education do you have?

____ d. What salary will you accept?

____ e. You are not going to get pregnant, are you?

____ f. Can you work on weekends?

____ g. Have you ever done this kind of work before?

____ h. What will you do if you have to work overtime every week for three months?

____ i. What do you think about working for a female supervisor?

____ j. Have you ever been arrested, and for what?

____ k. Can you take orders?

____ l. Can you think for yourself?

____ m. How sure are you that you will never miss a day's work?

____ n. Do you get bored easily?

____ o. Why do you want to work for us?

____ p. What kind of work have you done before?

____ q. Are you married or divorced?

____ r. How much do you drink?

____ s. Which shifts can you work?

____ t. To what clubs or associations do you belong?

____ u. Why should we hire you?

Why is it important to know the relevant questions that a personnel officer might ask you?

What are some other relevant questions that you might be asked in a job interview?

Exercise 6b

The Relevant Equation For Better Grades

Better grades and relevance have a lot to do with each other. An average course might contain 150,000 words in the text and lectures! The challenge for both student and instructor is to sort out the few words and the concepts behind them that are truly relevant. For the instructor this often means isolating the few powerful ideas he or she would like students to retain and use long after the course is over. For the students this often means predicting accurately what will be tested and then presenting this relevant knowledge effectively on the test.

In some ways this becomes a giant game. The instructor cannot simply list the few things out of those 150,000 words which are most relevant, because other things are important also (even if not as important). So he or she gives hints and clues as to what is most relevant, usually in the lectures. The student must listen for these clues, learn the right things for the tests and then learn how to be relaxed and controlled enough to focus on what is relevant during the test. Here is the equation:

Clues + Relevance + Control = Better Grades

Good instructor clues

+

Student alertness to relevance

+

Controlled student thoughts during tests

=

Better grades

The two activities in this exercise will help you master that equation while learning something about relevance in the process.

Instructors say many things in class. Some are relevant (for learning, studying and tests), and some are not. Here are some statements that an instructor in a study skills course might begin to make. Check the seven most relevant statements and be prepared to explain your choices. First, complete this sentence:

In this situation, relevant refers to anything that . . .

____ a. "It seems to me that many students just don't care any more. For example, ..."

____ b. "Three methods of notetaking — and this is important — are ..."

____ c. "Research shows that planning your time is one of the most important factors in your college success. Another important factor is ..."

____ d. "I don't like students who ..."

____ e. "I know it is hard for many students to study, especially when they have a family, a job, or ..."

____ f. "Three major writers on study skills are Walter Pauk, ..."

____ g. "A lot of what teachers lecture on is not really important, but they ..."

____ h. "Learning styles are defined as ..."

____ i. "Here are five things that good students usually do:"

____ j. "Tests that measure what you truly understand are hard to make up, hard to grade, and ..."

____ k. "It seems to me that the most important things to do when you listen to a lecture are ..."

____ l. "I sometimes wonder how many students are just in school for financial aid, or for ..."

____ m. "Usually I don't want students to memorize things, but in the case of these items ..."

____ n. "An example of good time management is setting aside a certain time each day to study, and then ..."

How do you know which of those items are most relevant? What are the clues that tell you when something in a lecture is important? See if you can list at least three reasons why you know which items are most relevant:

Reason # 1:

Reason # 2:

Reason # 3:

Why is it important to figure out what is relevant or not in a lecture? Give several reasons below.

Homework

Listen carefully to your instructor's lecture in another course. Heed the instructor's gestures, tone of voice. Listen for the key words he or she uses to warn you that something is relevant. On a separate sheet, write down at least three examples of those warning words, gestures and tones that you find in another class. Be exact about what was said, how it was conveyed, and how you knew it signalled relevance.

Having listened carefully to her study skills instructor's lectures, Suzanne is now taking one of the tests. Listed below are some of the thoughts running through her head while she takes the test. Some of them are relevant and some of them are distractions. The distractions hurt her confidence, take her mind off what she knows.

1. What do we mean by **relevant** here? Complete this statement:

   *In this situation **relevant** means a thought that will ...*

Next you will label each one of these thoughts and add a comment. Put an "R" in front of those that are relevant, and explain why they are relevant in the space after them. Put a "D" before those that are distractions and tell what she could do about them in the space below each. An example is given.

Are you ready? Are you sure you do not want to reread the instructions?

_____ a. "I'll begin by looking over the entire test to see what I have to do."

This helps her plan her time during the test.

_____ b. "Let me read over these directions again to make sure I understand what I'm supposed to do."

_____ c. "If I fail this one I won't pass the course."

_____ d. "I can't think of the answers. Maybe I'll get an idea from the next page."

_____ e. "This test is four pages long. I'll never finish all that by the end of the period!"

_____ f. "People are already through! And I'm still on the first page."

_____ g. "This guy next to me keeps coughing and it's driving me crazy."

____ h. "My teacher keeps walking by my desk. I'm sure she must think I'm cheating."

____ i. "Now that I'm finished I think I had better double-check to make sure I didn't leave out anything."

____ j. "I can't decide on this question. Let me see if I can narrow it down to two possible answers and then choose one of them."

____ k. "Oh, my heavens! Word problems! I just knew they would have math word problems. I'd better just give up on them and go on to the next type. I never could handle them."

2. Why is it important to be alert to what you are thinking while you are taking a test?

3. Distracting thoughts like some of those on the previous page are known as *negative self-talk.* Why do you think they are given that name?

4. Share your answers with others in the class, and add below any especially good answers which others suggest.

5. List at least three times that you find yourself using negative self-talk (putting yourself down or doubting yourself) and write down what effect it has on your actions, words or decisions.

Exercise 6c

Listening For Relevance On The Job

Imagine you are working during the summer at a fast food restaurant. You want to be a success so it will turn into a year-round job. Your supervisor talks a lot; you listen. You try to figure out what is relevant to your goal. Below are some of your supervisor's statements. Check the seven most relevant statements and be prepared to give your reasons.

First, complete this sentence:

In this situation, a relevant statement is one that ...

a. "There are either lots of people or none in here!"

b. "Angela is late again! That burns me up."

c. "You burned the fries. Why don't you watch the clock on the fry maker?"

d. "I sure get sick of smelling all this food sometimes."

e. "This fast-food chain pays lousy!"

f. "I would love an office job. If we make enough profit, maybe I'll get one."

g. "Be sure that the floor is clean and dry. That really keeps the customers coming back."

h. "That other fast-food place advertises that their people always smile. That's dumb! I'm sure all of you always smile, too."

i. "I appreciate people who solve problems themselves and don't always bring them to me."

j. "This parking lot is too small. At noon we are losing business because people can't find a place to park."

k. "If a hamburger is cooked for over 14 minutes, toss it."

l. "I love pizza. Maybe someday we will serve pizza here."

m. "Keep working like you are and you will have a job here forever."

Think About It!

Identify what Thinking Tools you have been using to come up with your answers about **relevance**.

Exercise 6d

Identifying Relevant Mathematics Information

Many textbook math word problems are very exact. They have just the right amount of information. You use everything and nothing is left over. Math problems outside the classroom are not like that. They are sloppy, with some information you use and some you do not. Sometimes important information is missing.

It is important to know what information is relevant and what information is not. These problems will help you with that. For each problem, draw a line through any information that you do not need. Here is an example:

> One-half of the people who applied for admissions to Dank University actually went there. The number of applicants in 1984 was 2,000. Almost 1,100 women applied. How many of the people who applied to Dank University in 1984 actually attended?

What information did you mark out? The final question asks how many actually attended. What information helps you answer that? The total of 2,000 people is certainly relevant. The fact that one-half actually went there is relevant. Is "almost 1,100 women" useful? It is interesting, but it does not help answer the question because the question does not ask about the number of women. Since it is not relevant, draw a line through the sentence, "Almost 1,100 women applied."

Now do the next six problems the same way. Draw a line through the information that is not relevant in answering the question. Be prepared to explain why it is not relevant.

1. One-half of the students at Burns College live on campus. If there are 2,600 students at Burns and 320 of them are freshmen, how many students live on campus?

2. How many 6-inch strips of wood can be cut from a length of wood 72 inches long and 2 inches wide?

3. Sam left home at 6:00 a.m. and drove 55 miles per hour for three hours to get to the beach. At what time did Sam get to the beach?

4. On the Latin test, Andrea scored 98. Eddie made four points less than Andrea. Sally made 10 points less than Eddie. What was Eddie's grade?

5. Mr. Carlton worked five hours overtime at $10 an hour. Mr. Cash worked a full week for $225 but no overtime. Mr. Adams worked a full week for $198 and 12 hours overtime at $10 an hour. How much overtime pay did Mr. Carlton and Mr. Adams make?

6. How many feet of fence would you buy to build a rectangular dog pen if the fence is to be 5 feet high, 12 feet long, 8 feet wide, with a 4-foot gate to be purchased separately?

All of the above problems had one piece of information that was not relevant. Outside the classroom, mathematics problems are not usually that predictable. The problems below are like that. They might have no irrelevant information, one piece of irrelevant information or two pieces of irrelevant information. Line out any irrelevant information. Good luck!

7. In a class of 30 students, the total number of points scored on a test was 2,160. What was the average grade on the test if each question counted two points?

8. Jeff drives his van to work each day and takes three riders who pay him $1 each day they ride. Tom only rode four days this week because he was sick one day. Chris rode five days and owed Jeff for three days last week. Ben rode two days and drove his own car three days; he spent $7 on gas for his car. Jeff used $15 worth of gas this week and $12 last week. Did he break even on this week's gas money?

9. Scott earns $1\frac{1}{4}$ days of sick leave each month. He has worked for two years and six months and has never missed a day for sickness. How many days of sick leave has he earned?

10. Eight secretaries had a bridal shower for Patsy, the daughter of their supervisor. They agreed to split the cost. They bought five quarts of punch for $1.50 per quart, two cans of nuts for $2.25 a can, four dozen brownies for $2.50 a dozen, and one of the girls contributed paper plates and napkins which she bought at a garage sale for $2 a year ago. How much did each secretary owe?

11. A recipe for brownies calls for one cup of sugar, one and one-half cups of milk and three-quarters of a cup of oil. It makes one pan of brownies, enough for six people. If you double the recipe, how many cups of liquid do you need?

12. Bigmobile advertises that its new sedan can travel 1,600 miles on one tank of gas. It gets 25 miles per gallon and has a special gas tank. If gas costs 75¢ per gallon and it costs $30 to fill the tank, how big is the tank?

Which of these problems were most difficult? Why?

Think About Word Problems

What have you learned about **thinking through math word problems?**

Exercise 6e

Relevance In Academic Advising

Hank's grades have been very poor for the last three semesters. His average is now below a C; he needs at least a C average to graduate. He is visiting his advisor to discuss his problem and possible solutions. Hank's advisor is weird. Sometimes she makes sense, and sometimes she does not. Below are some of the advisor's statements.

First, complete the following sentence:

*In this situation **relevant** means . . .*

Now check the eight statements you think are most relevant.
Explain why they are relevant in the spaces provided.

____ a. You have one quarter to raise your average, or you will be suspended.

____ b. I saw you talking to a bad bunch of students yesterday.

____ c. You should take only three carefully chosen courses next quarter.

____ d. Your brother graduated from here with honors.

____ e. Let's take a look at your work schedule.

____ f. What does your father do for a living?

____ g. Do you think that a tutor would help?

____ h. Did you go to the beach the first week in June?

____ i. Do you have a personal or physical problem that is interfering with your studying?

____ j. Have you considered another program of study that may not require as much academic background?

____ k. Another student told me you were real lazy in high school, too.

____ l. Let's look at your placement test scores.

____ m. Let's talk about why you are enrolled in college.

____ n. Are you on a basic grant?

What was the most important thing you had to do to complete this exercise?

Think about arguments and debates you have either been a part of or have witnessed. Have you been aware of irrelevant information being slipped into the conversation? Why do you think people do this? Is it done consciously or unconsciously?

Exercise 6f

Relevant Skills For Jobs Of The Future

Preparing for the future is confusing. Job duties, requirements and career ladders change rapidly. Experts indicate that the average college graduate will have at least five very different jobs during her or his working life. Many, if not most, of those now graduating from high school will work in jobs which are almost totally unlike jobs as they exist today.

If we assume that a main reason for seeking a college degree is to prepare for a rewarding career, then this type of future presents both instructors and students with a problem. How do we prepare for what does not yet exist? Below is a quotation about what many employers who foresee these future changes want of new graduates. Read it carefully.

> " It is impossible for business to know what their manpower needs will be in five or ten years. We do not know what specialties we will need. We do know that our needs will change quickly and education will lag behind. So our basic need is for people with general skills — basics like the 3R's, the ability to think, and other skills that can be used in many jobs. Give us new employees with those skills and we can, if absolutely necessary, teach them the rest."

This quotation is very relevant to you. In the space below, answer this question:

In what ways is that quotation relevant to you in college?

Share your answers with others and discuss them.

What skills will help you prepare for the kind of future in that quotation? Here are listed some skills. Check the eight or nine of them that you think will be most relevant in that future.

____ a. Taking shorthand.

____ b. Writing a computer program.

____ c. Taking notes in a lecture.

____ d. Typing well.

____ e. Leading a meeting.

____ f. Taking pictures.

____ g. Writing a technical report.

____ h. Taking orders.

____ i. Taking responsibility.

____ j. Figuring out what is wrong with a broken machine.

____ k. Interpreting a poem.

____ l. Following a set of written instructions.

____ m. Explaining technical things to a customer.

____ n. Operating a personal computer.

____ o. Planning and carrying out a job by yourself.

____ p. Solving problems.

____ q. Memorizing a list of spare parts.

____ r. Being the first to learn a new procedure.

____ s. Convincing a supervisor that you need a day off.

____ t. Reading a letter or memorandum.

____ u. Asking questions.

As a team, agree on and list below the letters of the eight skills you think will be most important in preparing you for that future.

List three skills not listed on the preceding page that will be relevant if you are to prepare for that type of future.

You have identified a few skills that will be most relevant to a world of jobs that continually change. Now try to narrow the list again. Pick out only three of those skills that are most relevant — the three you are sure you need to have. Then answer these questions about them.

Skill # 1:

1. What is it?

2. Why is it relevant?

3. Where and how can you learn it?

Skill # 2:

1. What is it?

2. Why is it relevant?

3. Where and how can you learn it?

Skill # 3:

1. What is it?

2. Why is it important?

3. Where and how can you learn it?

Think About It!

List a Thinking Tool that you are using now.

Finally, look at all the skills on the previous pages that you have identified as relevant. Answer these questions.

1. What are the relevant skills at which you think you are good?

2. What are the relevant skills you think you need to develop?

3. Where and how can you develop those latter skills?

Exercise 6g

Thinking Tools With Relevance

You have completed enough relevance exercises now to know that relevance is a complicated subject. Questioning relevance does not always yield a yes or no answer. More often your answer will be *maybe* or *it depends* or *a little bit.* Your Thinking Tools thus become very important. To know what relevance is you must have decided what the issue is, what aspects to consider, and generally what sorts of information you will need. Often you have to decide these things even before you have much information. That makes the thinking process complicated. Review earlier exercises if you wish. Then answer the questions below concerning the mental processes you use as you sort out the issue of relevance.

1. What are the three most important Thinking Tools you have used when working on relevance? Remember that you often get a sense of your direction and conclusions before seeking information that is useful in getting there. Remember that, when dealing with broad choices, you are considering the relevance and implications of several alternatives at the same time. Remember that you can't be certain about relevance without thinking first. What is your mind doing to cope with all of these uncertainties and possibilities? List the three most important Thinking Tools you use for relevance.

   1.

   2.

   3.

2. Now compare your list with the Thinking Tools other class members listed. What other ones did they suggest that you agree with? List them here.

3. Why do you think other people identified Thinking Tools that you did not list and that perhaps you still do not think are important? Check any of the following answers that you agree with.

____ They are not good thinkers.

____ I am not a good thinker.

____ They did not understand the question.

____ I did not understand the question.

____ They took the easy way out by just listing things.

____ I took the easy way out by just listing things.

____ Other reason(s) — specify what they are:

4. What are two or three important things that you have learned about relevance in this chapter?

a.

b.

c.

Supplemental Exercise 6h

Relevance In Finding A Place To Live

Imagine you are moving into a new town to take a job. You will be earning $1,100 a month. You are married and have one child. Your spouse (husband or wife) plans to continue college nearby. You need to find a place to live. Soon you find you have collected the information listed below. Check the eight items that are most relevant.

First, however, complete this sentence:

In this situation, ***relevance*** *means those things that ...*

____ a. There is a yellow house you really like. It is near your job, but it is not for sale.

____ b. A really great apartment area in town has a pool and rents an unfurnished one-bedroom apartment for $425 a month.

____ c. There is an old house for rent at $150 per month. It is 18 miles from your spouse's school and 30 miles from your job.

____ d. The want ads in the newspaper show some property for sale nearby. One parcel is 25 acres with a well but no house at $1,000 per acre.

____ e. Your aunt lives alone in a big house 40 miles from school and 42 miles from your job.

____ f. An apartment building is new, partly government funded and rents a one-bedroom apartment for $212 a month if you qualify. You do qualify, but there is a nine-month waiting list.

_____ g. Your car is deteriorating and needs many repairs.

_____ h. A farmer who lives 24 miles away wants someone to live on his farm and work the land fulltime for six months of the year. In exchange he will provide a house and garden free 12 months a year.

_____ i. Your grandmother likes brick houses.

_____ j. You really hate yard work.

_____ k. Your spouse does not want to live in a trailer or a tiny apartment.

_____ l. There are many real estate companies in the town.

_____ m. A 50-year-old, three-bedroom house is available for $31,000 on a half-acre lot.

_____ n. A government report shows that the price of housing is rising 9 percent every year.

_____ o. You hope to get a better job soon.

_____ p. You are very handy at making repairs but do not like to do it.

Think About It!

How do you know what is **relevant**?
What Thinking Tools did you use in deciding?

Supplemental Exercise 6i

One Day In The Life Of George

Sometimes relevance does not occur in small pieces. We need to see big patterns of human behavior in order to identify what is and is not relevant. Here is part of the life of a student named George. Read it carefully and then answer the questions about relevance in his life.

George was required to take developmental courses before he could take certain technical courses in his program of study. He completed the prerequisite developmental courses and has begun a new quarter in his main course work determined to try hard and make it.

On the day of registration, George was invited to go skiing at the lake with some old high school friends. He really wanted to go and decided to register late.

Since he registered late George missed his first class period in Introduction to Data Processing. He found some other students who were in the course, however, and got the reading assignment for the next class period. When he went to buy his books he realized he did not have enough money to buy the math workbook. George decided he probably could manage without it; he had done well in his developmental math course.

George made his second class, English Composition, with five minutes to spare. He had a few extra minutes to chat with some of the other people in the class and realized he knew some of them from high school or from developmental courses.

Some of the other students knew the instructor and warned George that he had better do very well on his beginning paragraph or he might have to go back into a developmental writing class. George thought hard about the topic the instructor assigned before beginning his paper. He jotted down his ideas and planned his paper carefully before beginning to write. He wrote his first draft, edited it, wrote his final draft in ink. He felt pleased with his paragraph.

The instructor suggested that the students begin keeping a journal, writing in it for at least 10 minutes each day. George was still working at Polksburgh Gas Station from 4:00 until midnight so he figured that since it was not required he would let the journal slide.

After English class a couple of guys invited George to join them for lunch. They went out for pizza and beer, and the waitress was very busy. They were late getting back for their afternoon class. George had located the classroom earlier in the day so at least he knew where he was supposed to be. Some of the other guys could not find their schedules. George thought, "How stupid!"

When George walked into his accounting class that afternoon the instructor was finishing up his explanation of the course and all that would be required. George found an extra copy of the course syllabus and quickly skimmed over it trying to figure out what the teacher was talking about.

At about the time George was finding his place in the syllabus, the instructor started lecturing from Chapter 1. George had not had a chance to look at the chapter since he had just bought his books that morning. Many of the ideas and concepts in the lecture were very new to George, and he did not know how to spell all the words the instructor used.

George began to have trouble following the lecture because he felt very sleepy. He began watching the clock at 3:00, realizing that if this instructor did not wind down soon George would be late for work. He never dreamed the class would last the whole period on the first day, and he did not have his uniform with him.

George was worried. He would never have time to get home and back to work on time. While he was trying to figure out what to do, the teacher gave the assignment for the next class. George missed it. He would have to get it later even though he had not had a chance to meet any of the other students and did not recognize anyone. Maybe the assignment was in the syllabus; he was in a hurry to get out of there.

George felt bad about his first day. He could see that he would need to do more homework than he had expected. He decided he should talk to his boss about working fewer hours. Maybe he should bring his uniform to school with him to save time in the afternoons.

It seemed like a tough deal. When was he going to have time to read the chapter for Introduction to Data Processing? He remembered that his first class was not until 10:30 the next day, so he decided he would go to campus early and study in the library. He was determined that he was going to make it this time — if only he could remember what the accounting instructor had said to do! "What was his name, anyway? And where is his office?" George pondered as he went to work.

1. Which of George's actions were relevant to his purpose of "making it"? List them here.

2. Which actions were harmful or clearly irrelevant to George's purpose?

3. What could George have done differently in each case where his actions were harmful or irrelevant?

4. Why do people often say one thing and then do another?

Exercise 6j

A Look At Relevance In Research

Writing a college-level research paper is difficult for many students. Why? There are at least three main reasons. First is the problem of what information to include as relevant or exclude as irrelevant. Second is the problem of organizing the information once you decide what to include. Third is the fact that many students do not realize that thoughtful writers of research papers keep going back and forth between the first two factors. This exercise focuses particularly on how to think through the first factor, relevant information, and a bit of the third factor. You will encounter the second factor, organizing information, later.

1. Imagine that your English instructor has assigned a paper. You are to write on the advantages and disadvantages of college football. You mention the subject to some friends while sitting in the cafeteria, and they start arguing about it. You listen and jot down some notes about what they are saying. Your notes are listed below. Check the items you think are relevant for your paper. Then pick five of them and explain why each is relevant in the space after the items.

    ____ a. Scholarships are awarded to attract good students.

    ____ b. Football players are stupid jocks.

    ____ c. Athletes never have to study.

____ d. Recruitment practices for athletes have gotten out of hand.

____ e. Cheerleaders are chosen based on popularity.

____ f. Colleges spend too much money on athletics; they should spend more on academics.

____ g. Athletic events bring money and students to a college.

____ h. Colleges with good football teams have a lot of school spirit.

____ i. Players who do well in college may become professionals.

____ j. There is a lot of drinking at football games.

____ k. Parking at the stadium is a big problem.

____ l. Good coaches teach leadership and discipline.

____ m. Football games are more popular than basketball games.

____ n. It is hard to get a date if you are not a football player.

____ o. Football heroes have a hard time adjusting to the real world after their college days are over.

____ p. Playing football improves one's physical condition.

____ q. Football is a form of entertainment for all students.

Do you think that others will agree with your ideas about what is relevant or not? Share your conclusions with others; be prepared to explain why you thought they were relevant or not.

2. In this situation Sarah is writing a paper on how she decided to major in business administration. First she thought up some ideas of her own. Then she asked a good friend to suggest some other things she might discuss. Here are their lists:

   Sarah thought of these things:

   ____ a. Worked in the office of a shipping company in high school.

   ____ b. Father taught math.

____ c. Liked accounting courses.

____ d. Good organizational skills.

____ e. Would like to own and operate a gift shop.

____ f. Artistic.

____ g. Won the history award in the ninth grade.

____ h. Enjoys working with people.

Her friend suggested these things:

____ i. Attended career day and enjoyed talking to business people.

____ j. Mother was a housewife.

____ k. Aptitude tests and interest surveys show that business would be a good major.

____ l. Best friend is majoring in business.

____ m. Economics teacher in high school thought Sarah caught on faster than all of the other students.

Now Sarah has many ideas to work with. Her second step is to decide which of those items are most relevant. Put an "R" before any ideas in the lists above that you think are especially relevant. Do that now.

Stop!

What does **relevant** mean in this case?

You have assessed some items, decided what **relevant** means, decided which items are relevant to writing the paper. Your last job is to **organize** the relevant items. Group them and decide on the order in which you will cover them in the paper. Use the space below to organize these ideas.

3. Now you must organize a research paper. You will do this in several steps.

Step 1

As a team, pick one of the two topics below for your paper or choose a third topic of your own choice.

____ The advantages of a teenager having his or her own car.

____ Reasons for choosing to come to this college.

____ Another topic (write it here):

Step 2

As a team, brainstorm about the topic and list your ideas here.

Step 3

As a team, decide which of these ideas (up to a maximum of 12) are most relevant and put a checkmark before them.

Step 4

As a team, organize the relevant ideas. Arrange them in an order that makes sense to you.

Step 5

As a team, list at least three relevant questions you would like to ask your instructor about this topic and paper before writing it.

You have now looked at the question of relevant information for a research paper. You have also struggled a little bit with the need to organize that information. At the beginning of this exercise we talked about three factors that make it difficult for many students to write research papers. Two of them are the difficulties of picking out relevant information and of organizing that information. The third is the fact that these first two are very interactive — one affects the other, then reacts to changes in the other, then again changes the other, and on and on.

Novice researchers usually use only two steps. First they gather a great deal of information and then stop their research. They then try to organize all that information by cramming all or most of it into the paper whether it fits or not.

Skilled, thoughtful researchers do not do this. They first get a general idea of what the paper will cover and how it will be organized. That tells them roughly what **relevance** is for their paper — information that fits the planned coverage and organization. Then they go out and collect the information they need based on that original idea of what is probably relevant.

Next, skilled researchers compare what they have learned with their original organizational plan. Almost always, they change the scope and organization to fit their new information. This change redefines **relevant information,** and more information is needed. So they research again and find more information, being more sure this time about what information they need. As they keep going back and forth, the organization becomes clearer and the information more relevant. Skilled researchers keep switching back and forth between relevant information and organizing schemes until they have a cohesive paper.

Find a topic you know very little about. Write a two-page paper on that topic. As you write it, practice the technique described above:

a. roughly organize

b. research relevant information

c. reorganize

d. find more relevant information

e. complete organizing and research

f. write

You do not have to write the paper. You can just submit your final organizational plan and your relevant information. By that time, however, you may discover it is so easy to write the paper that you will want to go ahead and do it. Organizing and collecting relevant information make writing your paper easier.

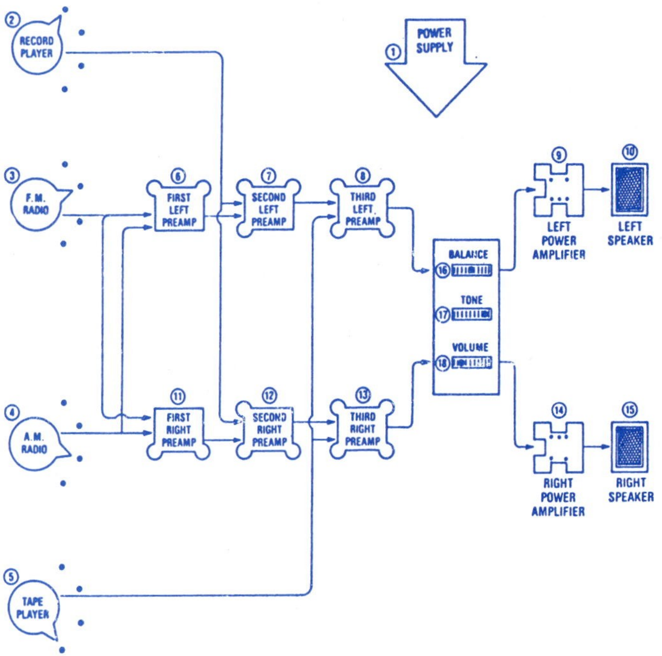

Stereo System

Supplemental Exercise 6k

Relevant Troubleshooting Of A Stereo System

Here again is the stereo system you worked with in the last chapter. If you have forgotten how it works, reread those pages. This time you will have to figure out what parts are relevant or not relevant to test in simulated stereo problems.

Many people waste money having repairmen check things that could not possibly be broken. Careful consumers think before they act — they think about what might be relevant to a problem before they try to fix it or pay someone else to fix it. If your car will not start, it is not relevant to test for a flat tire because a flat tire could not cause a car not to start. If your lawn mower will run only at full speed, but not at a slow speed, then you do not need to check the gas. Something is wrong, but if you are thoughtful you know it has gas because it runs at full speed. Try using this same kind of thinking with this problem-ridden stereo system.

1. You turn on the stereo with the switch turned to the tape player. No sound comes from either speaker, but the lights on the dials come on. Check the numbers of all the parts that are relevant to check in this situation.

_____ 1	_____ 5	_____ 9	_____ 13	_____ 17
_____ 2	_____ 6	_____ 10	_____ 14	_____ 18
_____ 3	_____ 7	_____ 11	_____ 15	
_____ 4	_____ 8	_____ 12	_____ 16	

Now discuss the answers with your team or the whole class. Did you miss any parts that should have been labeled with an "R"? If so, list them below and explain why those parts are relevant.

I should have marked # _____ as relevant because:

I should have marked # _____ as relevant because:

2. This time you turn the stereo on with the switch on FM radio. No sound comes from the right speaker, but the left speaker is very loud. Check the numbers of the stereo parts that are relevant to test in this situation.

_____ 1	_____ 5	_____ 9	_____ 13	_____ 17
_____ 2	_____ 6	_____ 10	_____ 14	_____ 18
_____ 3	_____ 7	_____ 11	_____ 15	
_____ 4	_____ 8	_____ 12	_____ 16	

Again, compare your answers with others in your class. Did you miss any that you should have checked? List and explain them below:

I should have marked # _____ as relevant because:

I should have marked # _____ as relevant because:

I should have marked # _____ as relevant because:

3. Now you turn on the stereo with the switch set for the record player. The right speaker cuts in and out while the left speaker has no sound at all. What could be the problem? Check all of the stereo parts you might want to test in this situation.

_____ 1	_____ 5	_____ 9	_____ 13	_____ 17
_____ 2	_____ 6	_____ 10	_____ 14	_____ 18
_____ 3	_____ 7	_____ 11	_____ 15	
_____ 4	_____ 8	_____ 12	_____ 16	

Compare your answers with others. Circle any answers in the list above that you should have checked but did not. Be sure you know **why** they are relevant.

Think About It!

What are you thinking about as you try to solve these problems?

Write down your mental activities.

Chapter Seven

Taking Risks Thoughtfully

Learning is a risky business. We take chances when we study and answer questions (or don't). Clever students have learned to be thoughtful risk-takers, weighing possible consequences against probabilities.

Everyone takes risks from the moment he starts making conscious choices. A three-year-old who glances both ways before dashing across the street to get a ball is taking a risk. The businesswoman who enters the fourteenth airplane on which she has flown this week is taking a risk. The student takes a risk when he puts down his book, deciding he has studied enough for the test. A driver takes a risk when he runs a yellow light. A woman takes a risk if she is the first to say "I love you" to a man. Life is a constant flow of risks.

Even though we all take risks, few of us have ever stopped to think about what a risk is. A risk refers to the chances that something negative will happen if you make a certain choice and take a certain action. Risks have two parts: a possible negative consequence, and the probability that the consequence will happen. Or, to put it another way:

Risk = Possible Negative Consequence + Probability

When determining the risks in a certain situation, we often ask what unpleasant outcome might occur. Then we ask what the chances are that the negative outcome will happen.

All of us have heard of a **high-risk situation**. What does it mean? A high-risk situation is one in which the probability is high that a negative consequence will occur. What, then, is a **low-risk situation?** It is one in which the probability is low that a negative consequence will occur. The only difference between a high-risk and a low-risk situation is the probability of something negative happening.

Think about that last sentence again. Consider buying a car as an example. If you buy any car, a possible negative consequence is that it might be a lemon. That is true of a brand new Mercedes (at over $30,000) and of a 15-year-old Volkswagen bug (at $200). Any car can be a lemon.

What is the difference, then, between buying a new Mercedes and a used VW? Only the probabilities. Either could be a lemon, but the probability that a new car will be a lemon is much lower than the probability that a used car will be a lemon. In terms of being mechanically unreliable, a new car is low risk and a used car is high risk. The probability is greater with a used car.

Think about crossing a road. Whenever you cross a road, there is a possibility you will be hit by a car. If you cross a street in a quiet subdivision, the possibility exists, but the odds are very low. If you cross an interstate highway, the same possibility exists, but the odds are much higher. It is a higher risk.

There is another aspect of risk-taking to consider. How much risk is too much? That depends partly on your personality and values. However, it also depends partly on the type of negative consequence which might occur. Assume that someone pays you $500 to take a risk. Would you do it? It would depend on the risk.

If you were challenged to take an examination without studying, you might judge that, although the probability of failing that test was 50 percent, this possible consequence was not too severe (You could still pass the course). You might take that risk for $500. But if the challenge involved even a 10 percent chance of losing your life, you probably would not take that risk. The probability in the second case would be far less, but the nature of the consequence would be very different! Risk-taking depends on the possible consequences.

People tend to use one of three basic types of risk-taking strategies. They tend to usually do one of these three things when faced with a risky choice.

The optimistic strategy

The person who uses the optimistic strategy expects the best possible consequence from his or her choice regardless of the probabilities of something bad happening. This type of person is the gambler, the confident person, the one who wants the best. With this strategy the person focuses on the best possible outcome and mainly ignores the negative possibilities.

The pessimistic strategy

The person using the pessimistic strategy seeks to avoid the worst possible consequences even at the cost of giving up something really good. This strategy seeks to avoid the unpleasant consequences and generally ignores the possible positive outcomes as well.

The safe strategy

When the safe strategy is used, the person is generally trying to find some middle ground which limits the probability that something bad will happen even if he must give up very positive outcomes also. This strategy abandons the best and worst possible consequences in order to pursue something in the middle.

With these three definitions in mind, think about your own choices and actions. What is your usual risk-taking strategy? Complete this statement in the space following it.

My Usual Risk-Taking Strategy Is:

The previous discussion sets the stage for this chapter. By the time you have satisfactorily completed the chapter, you will be able to do the following:

- ❑ Identify probabilities in choice situations.
- ❑ List and apply three risk-taking strategies.
- ❑ Judge the reliability of information when taking risks.
- ❑ Analyze your personal values in risk-taking circumstances.

Risk-taking is a routine but complicated human activity. The exercises in this chapter deal with certain key aspects. Following are some other aspects of risk-taking which you ought to keep in mind.

1. Risk-taking basically deals with cause-and-effect relationships. When we take risks, we consciously or unconsciously speculate that "If I do this, then these are the odds that the other thing might happen." Everything you learned about cause-and-effect earlier in this book is helpful in thinking about risk-taking.

2. Risk-taking varies with the individual and the situation. As you have seen, the stakes are higher in some situations (failing a test versus losing your life). Those stakes certainly affect the risks you will take. Also, some people are more willing to take risks in a given situation than other people. Sometimes they are just more willing to take greater risks. Sometimes the particular thing at stake means more to them than it does to others.

3. Risk-taking is a learned behavior. You have learned to be the type of risk-taker you are; it is not unchangeable. If at some point your risk-taking strategy no longer works, you can change it.

4. Individuals are not consistent in their risk-taking strategies. You may take more risks when you are fresh and happy, and less risks when you are tired or depressed. We are usually fairly consistent in our risk-taking but not always.

5. Individuals use different risk-taking strategies in different situations. Someone who is an optimistic risk-taker in social situations (being a leader, asking someone out on a date, and so forth) might be very pessimistic in academic situations (not using new learning strategies, not writing what they actually think on a test).

There are two other important aspects of risk-taking. One is your ability to weigh the reliability of the information you have, its solidity in terms of taking a risk based on that information. The other depends on your values, what things are important to you when taking risks. These will be dealt with later in this chapter.

Remember this about risk-taking:

- ❑ deals with cause-and-effect relationships.
- ❑ varies with the individual and the situation.
- ❑ is a learned behavior.
- ❑ individuals are inconsistent in their risk-taking.
- ❑ different situations require different risk-taking.

Exercise 7a

Risking A Change Of Learning Strategy

Jack has never been very successful in school. It has always been hard for him to catch onto new things. Maybe that is because he has never been very interested in school. Therefore, he has developed his own way to get by on tests.

Jack memorizes. He studies lists of facts, words, dates, people and theories. He spends a lot of time doing this and it has usually gotten him through his courses. He made D's and C's in high school, but sometimes he even made a B when an instructor only asked multiple choice questions.

Now Jack is enrolled at Mountain State College. Two of his courses are basic reading and basic mathematics. These are courses where everybody learns at his or her own pace. Jack is making progress in those courses.

His other two courses, however, are Introduction to Business and General Psychology. He is failing both of them, after only a month of classes. Both instructors give weekly quizzes with essay, discussion and other forms of open-ended questions. Jack's technique of listing memorized facts does not work on these tests. The instructors say they want broader answers, general ideas.

Jack is confused about what to do. He thinks that the answer is to memorize facts more completely, write a little more neatly. His advisor says that Jack needs to learn a different way of studying and taking tests. Jack is scared of that idea. He says it is unnecessary and argues that his strategy of memorizing has gotten him to college and should keep working. Jack is beginning to doubt this will work, though.

1. What possibilities does Jack have? List them, and rate each one as "very risky," "risky" or "not very risky."

   - ❑
   - ❑
   - ❑

2. What would Jack do if he used each risk-taking strategy?

   a. Optimistic?

   b. Pessimistic?

   c. Safe?

3. For the optimistic and pessimistic strategies, what would he want or fear most?

   a. With the optimistic strategy, he would want:

   b. With the pessimistic strategy, he would want to avoid:

4. What should Jack do? Why?

5. If you think Jack should learn a different way of studying:

   a. How should he learn to study differently?

   b. Where could he learn how to do that?

6. Why is Jack scared of learning to study a different way?

7. What kind of risk-taker do you think Jack is in school?

What Thinking Tools do you use to decide on the **level of a risk**?

Exercise 7b

Risk-Taking For A College Student

Patrick has a problem. He has run out of money. He works a part-time job at a car wash. He is on his own — he moved out of his parents' house when they objected to his late hours and the nights he did not come home at all. He has spent all of his federal grant money. Now the instructor in his program of study (engineering graphics) is demanding that he buy an expensive ($244) drawing set. Most of Patrick's classmates bought it months ago.

Patrick's grades are falling because he does not have the set. He is thinking about trying to work more hours at the car wash, but even now he barely has time for studying, school and going out with his friends. He could sell his car, but then he would have to depend on his friends to get him to school and work every day. He could try not paying his rent for a while but suspects that his landlady already does not like him.

1. List five possible actions that Patrick could take which might solve or ease his problem.

   a.

   b.

c.

d.

e.

2. Rank the possible actions above in terms of risks. The one you mark "5" is the most risky action, and the one you mark "1" is the least risky action. Mark them in the spaces in front of them.

3. Be sure you remember what a risk is. Write below, in your own words, what a risk is.

4. Describe below the negative consequences that are likely to happen with the possibilities you marked as highest-risk (5, 4 and 3) in the list.

   a. Negative consequence of action rated # 5:

   b. Negative consequence of action rated #4:

   c. Negative consequence of action rated #3:

5. What choice would you make in that situation?

6. Why would you make that choice?

7. Discuss your answers with others in the class.

Exercise 7c

Risk-Taking In A Job Situation

Mac works in the supply department of a computer assembly plant. He and another person, Harry, started working there at about the same time, six months ago. Mac has become friendly with three or four of the old hands, while Harry spends most of his extra time with the supervisor's sister, who works in another department. Recently, an audit revealed that a number of expensive ($75 each) computer chips are missing — they have disappeared gradually over a period of several months.

This has never happened before, and there is talk that one of the new workers is stealing them. Mac thinks that the supervisor has looked intently at him for the past two days. Mac knows he is innocent, but he is worried that he could end up getting blamed — and fired.

1. List five actions that Mac could take, and rate them 1 to 5 (with 5 being most risky, 1 being least risky).

   ❑

   ❑

   ❑

   ❑

   ❑

2. Do you remember the discussion of risk-taking strategies in the Introduction to this chapter? Reread it if necessary. Then answer these questions.

   a. What action would you take if you were using a pessimistic risk-taking strategy (avoiding the worst)?

   b. What action would you take with an optimistic risk-taking strategy (going for the best)?

   c. What action would you take with a safe strategy (balance the worst and best)?

3. What was the worst possibility that you wanted to avoid with your pessimistic strategy (2a) above?

4. What was the best possibility that you wanted to go for with your optimistic strategy (2b) above?

5. What would you do in this situation? Explain why.

Think About Risks

How do the Thinking Tools used in **testing possibilities** help you decide what risk-taking strategy to follow?

Exercise 7d

Determining Reliability With Risk-Taking

Whenever we do something that involves a degree of risk, we must consider the **reliability** of the information we have. Reliability means dependability. How sure are we that the information is accurate? Can we trust the source to be honest, objective, unbiased and informed in this situation? A person who is a very reliable source of information in one situation may not be reliable in another. Your reliable auto mechanic may not be someone you want to depend on for advice about flowers, history, or investments. Reliability depends on the situation.

In the exercise on the following pages, some possible sources of information are listed first, followed by some choice situations. For each choice situation, select the **most reliable sources** which would help you make the best choice. Find as many sources as would be helpful and reliable for each choice situation. List the letters of the reliable sources in front of each choice.

For example, consider what sources of information would and would not be reliable in this case.

❑ If you are considering dropping out of school, then:

- discussing it with your counselor (b), talking to your academic advisor (i), and talking to your family (l) would be ways to get reliable information

- asking the librarian (a), consulting a lawyer (g), or talking to a waitress or bartender (j) would not be ways to get reliable information.

Which Of These Would Be Reliable Sources Of Information? ...

a. Ask the librarian.

b. Discuss it with your counselor.

c. Make a list of pros and cons from things you remember.

d. Read about it in newspapers and magazines.

e. Discuss it with your teacher.

f. Think about your personal preferences — what you like and dislike.

g. Consult a lawyer.

h. Ask a friend with experience.

i. Talk to your academic advisor.

j. Ask a waitress or bartender.

k. Visit appropriate places.

l. Talk to your family.

m. Check credit references.

n. Watch programs on TV about it.

o. Consult consumer guides.

p. Talk to a recruiter.

q. Talk to salespersons.

r. Read catalogs, brochures, etc.

s. Talk to a data processing instructor.

t. Check employment agencies.

u. Talk to your minister.

v. Look in the Yellow Pages.

… In These Choice Situations?

A. Ordering a meal in a restaurant.

B. Voting for candidates in a major election.

C. Buying a home computer.

D. Selecting a college.

E. Choosing where to go for a vacation.

F. Selecting courses to take next term.

G. Accepting or rejecting a job offer.

H. Financing the sale of your home or not to your cousin who wants to buy it.

I. Dropping a course or not in the middle of the term.

J. Deciding whether to join the Army, get a job, or go to school.

1. After making your choices above, discuss them with others in the class. Use the following questions to guide your discussion; make notes of your answers.

   a. On which questions was there the most disagreement?

   b. Did the disagreements seem to rise more from questions of fact, interpretation or personal preference?

c. Were there one or two sources which seemed reliable in most of those choice situations? If so, which ones?

d. How would you complete this sentence?
Reliable sources of information are those which ...

2. Pick five of the sources of information which were not especially useful in the original ten items earlier in this exercise. For each one, list one type of choice where that source would be very reliable and useful.

- For example, *u. Talk to your minister* would be a reliable and useful source of information when selecting a wedding date.

-

-

-

-

Exercise 7e

Risking A Friendship

Molly is often put on the spot by her good friend, June. For example, last night June did not do her French homework because she went out to a party instead. Molly is certain that this morning June will ask to borrow Molly's homework, just to get started. Molly also knows that June copied her homework, word for word, the last time this happened.

Barbara Abrams, the French teacher, told both students they would receive an F for that homework assignment because although June turned in a good paper, she couldn't answer any questions about it. Molly does not want June to get into trouble. She also does not want to spoil their friendship because she cares about June. Also, June is very popular on campus and includes Molly in many of her activities. Molly is a little scared of June, too. June is known to hold a grudge. Molly has observed this herself from watching run-ins that June has had with other people.

Molly does not think it is fair for her to get F's on homework assignments just to help June out. Professor Abrams has always been very fair and considerate of Molly. She commended Molly for her work in her first French course; Molly earned an A. She is also advisor for the French Honor Society, and Molly is the president.

So Molly is left with her choice: should she or should she not let June borrow her homework "just to get started" when June asks for it this morning?

1. What should Molly do?

   List as many possibilities as you can, and then rate each one as "very risky" (VR), "risky" (R), or "not very risky" (NVR).

2. Decide what Molly would do if she were using different risk-taking strategies:

   - A pessimistic risk-taking strategy?

   - An optimistic risk-taking strategy?

   - A safe risk-taking strategy?

3. The issues of reliability and relevance are more difficult in personal situations like Molly's than in impersonal situations like buying a TV. Below, list six key pieces of relevant information Molly has. Then rate the reliability of each piece of information. Two examples are given.

- June holds a grudge.
  Reliable, because Molly has seen her do it.

- June will just borrow Molly's homework "to get started."
  Not reliable, because June has lied about that in the past.

-

-

-

-

-

-

4. What would you do if you were Molly?

5. Why would that be Molly's best course of action?

6. Share your answers with others and discuss them. After you discuss them, answer these questions:

    a. When we judge the reliability of information before taking a risk, are we actually judging the information itself?

    b. If not, what are we judging?

Exercise 7f

Weighing Relevance And Reliability When Taking Risks

Reliability, as you learned in the last exercise, means how accurate and complete your information is. Reliable information is information you can trust and take a risk with because the source is credible in that situation. Earlier in this book, you discussed relevant information; information can be reliable, relevant, both or neither in a given situation.

Stop and think about that last sentence for a moment before proceeding.

- If information is **reliable but not relevant**, what does that mean?

It means that the source gives you accurate information, but the information is not helpful in that situation.

Example

You are trying to get your TV repaired for under $30, and the TV store owner says he has a special deal on new 19" color TVs for only $345.

- If information is **relevant but not reliable**, what does that mean?

It means that the information is useful in that situation, but it may not be accurate.

Example

Your 9-year-old cousin says that you can get your TV fixed for no more than $25.

- If information is **not reliable and not relevant**, what does that mean?

It means that the information is neither useful nor trustworthy.

Example

You are trying to get your TV fixed, and the TV repairman gives you a good tip on a horse race.

- If the information is **relevant and reliable**, what does that mean?

It means it is useful and trustworthy.

Example

The TV store owner says that he will have your TV fixed and ready for under $25 by tomorrow morning.

With all of this in mind, consider the following situation. Your TV is broken, but this time you decide to buy a new one. Your cousin Charlie, who is kind of slow at times, says he has a lot of information about televisions. Although you doubt Charlie has any good information, you ask him to give you what he knows. He drops by your house the next day, and it is obvious that not all of the information is equally good. In order to make use of it, you have to decide on the relevance and reliability of each part.

Rank each item of information below on both relevance and reliability. If it is very relevant or reliable, put a ✔. If it is not very relevant or reliable, leave it blank. Be prepared to explain your answer. An example is given.

Note: This information is made up. Do not try to buy a TV on the basis of this information.

Very Relevant	Very Reliable	
______	✓	1. *Consumer Reports* rates Zenith first in company profits.
______	______	2. The Better Business Bureau says that Buy-Now TV Company has been reported for high pressure salesmanship.
______	______	3. The salesman at JGF Company (which sells TVs) said he would not own a Sony TV (which his company does not sell).
______	______	4. Mr. Clanks, a TV repairman, owns a GE television.
______	______	5. *Consumer Reports* rates RCA last for ease of repair.
______	______	6. Mr. Green, who knows a lot of things, says JGF Company will have a good sale on TVs in two months.
______	______	7. Color City TVs advertises a special offer — a free toaster or coffee pot with a purchase of $750 or more.
______	______	8. Buy It For More Company, which sells GE televisions, has opened its own service department.
______	______	9. *Consumer Reports* says that RCA color TVs have the best color of any set and also give off x-rays.

Very Relevant	Very Reliable	
______	______	10. The clerk at Tri-City TV Sales says that they give R&D Red Stamps with each TV.
______	______	11. *Business Weekly* states that Sony is a Japanese firm.
______	______	12. Watch 'Em TV advertises that it gives a one-month subscription to cable TV free when you buy any RCA console.
______	______	13. Tri-City TV Sales says that it has no service repairmen.
______	______	14. You have decided you cannot afford to pay more than $300 for a TV.
______	______	15. *Consumer Reports* found problems with Zenith's solid-state circuitry.
______	______	16. Buy Now TVs is advertising a sale of GE television sets.
______	______	17. The Better Business Bureau has received fewer complaints about Color City TVs than any other TV dealer in town.
______	______	18. The newspaper says there is a Navy football game on TV on Saturday.

Very Relevant	Very Reliable	
______	______	19. Ms. Phelps, an elementary school teacher, recommends that everyone buy a Philco TV.
______	______	20. Color City TV's salesmen rank RCA first and GE second. These are the only two brands they sell.
______	______	21. Mr. Clanks, a TV repairman, says that parts for Zenith TVs are easy to get.
______	______	22. The man down the street says he had to buy a new antenna when he bought a GE TV right after he moved in.
______	______	23. Watch 'Em TV advertises that they have the smallest finance charge in town on its sets. They carry RCA and Zenith.
______	______	24. *Consumer Reports* says that Sony has the best remote control system.
______	______	25. Your best friend Fred, who is a truck driver, says that he would never buy a foreign TV set.

Discuss your answers with others, and be prepared to explain your answers.

Balancing relevance and reliability is confusing, isn't it? Below, write down at least two reasons why it is important to be sure of both of them before making a risky decision.

a.

b.

Think About It!

How do Thinking Tools help you "juggle" both **reliability** and **relevance** in your mind at the same time?

Exercise 7g

Risk-Taking And Values

We have explored three aspects of risk-taking: probabilities of consequences, risk-taking strategies, and the reliability and relevance of information. All three are important, but there is one more very important factor to consider: our values. Values identify those ideas, situations, feelings, or products which are important to us. We may value privacy, friendship, independence, honesty. We make choices and take risks in ways which lead towards those things we value.

Values are very general words. They are labels for broad concepts or topics. The specific choices we make based on our values are not statements of the values themselves; they are merely examples of the values we hold. A businesswoman who dresses conservatively may value professional respect; a student who always wears jeans and a t-shirt may value convenience. In each case, the clothes are only an example of the value. Here is another example of a general value and several actions that might be taken by someone who held that value.

Value: Security

Actions: Lock doors at night.

Find jobs where there is little chance of being fired.

Save part of the paycheck regularly.

Never gamble or buy stocks and bonds.

Each of those actions says something about the person's values. They all involve being sure, playing it safe. They all suggest a value which might be called security. Values are abstract ideas represented by the concrete things we show to be important through our actions and choices.

Here are other important elements of values and how they affect the risks we take:

1. *Each of us has many values.* There are many things that are important to us which influence our choices and actions. A mother may value life very much, but may also value joy, freedom, and "my children's happiness". All of us have many values.

2. *Values often conflict.* A student may value being honest at the same time she values academic success or good grades. Does she tell the professor what she really thinks about a particular topic when she knows her opinion differs from his? Her two values conflict in that situation.

   Very often a problem consists almost totally of a conflict between our values. Someone else may not have a problem in that same situation because his values do not conflict. Our many values often get in the way of each other when we try to make a choice.

3. *Our values are clearest in our actions, not in our words.* It is easy — and human — to say we value things our society accepts as good. Often, however, our actions say something else. A man may say that he values family. If he spends all of his non-working hours hunting, golfing, drinking, doing church work or other activities instead of being with his family, then his actions speak louder than his words. What he says he values, and what he really values, are not the same thing.

What, then, are values? They are general labels for the things we believe and act upon as important. Here are some statements of values:

- Independence
- Security
- Family
- Professional Respect
- Acceptance By Others
- Job Satisfaction
- Power/Influence
- Freedom
- Honesty
- Companionship
- Excitement
- Peacefulness

Values are very important parts of risk-taking. We will take bigger risks for some values than for others. We will avoid taking risks in order to protect those values. We can fully understand our risk-taking tendencies only when we understand our values.

As has been mentioned, we often say one thing and do another; we deceive ourselves. How do we know what we sincerely value? There are three stages in the process of discovering our true values.

a. Look at an action or choice and the reason for making it a certain way.

Example

Declining to go out with friends because you have some work to do.

b. Figure out what value(s) that reason suggests.

One possible value might be:
fulfilling my responsibilities

Another possible value could be:
being by myself

c. See if you can identify other actions that reflect that value. Remember that a value is a general label for many different specific actions. You should be able to discover many such actions for an important value.

If you find supporting actions for the possibility that you value "fulfilling my responsibilities", this suggests it is a true value. But perhaps you uneasily recall many times when you read a book instead of doing your homework, or walked away from urgent tasks at work just because it was time to leave. You might actually not value fulfilling your responsibilities. Perhaps your choice of not going out with friends reflected instead another value: "being by myself." Again, seek past actions which reflect that being by yourself is important to you.

The exercise on the following page helps you identify a value and then seek supporting evidence for it. Follow the three steps discussed above: (a) choose an action (on the left side); (b) think about what value it might reflect and write it in the middle; and (c) "prove it" by listing two or three other actions a person might take which would also reflect that value. The first one is done as an example.

	If I choose this action:	Then I might value this:	Other evidence in my life:
1.	If you were failing a course, would you:	Take the easy way out.	Lie when caught in a situation that is embarrassing.
	a. Get tutoring.		
XX	b. Drop it.		Cheat if I can.
	c. Study harder.		
			Pretend not to hear someone needing help.
2.	Faced with temptation, do you:		
	a. Think what your parents would say or do.		
	b. Judge the pros and cons for yourself.		
	c. Worry about what others think.		
3.	If you apply for a job and your best friend gets it, would you:		
	a. Congratulate him.		
	b. Avoid him.		
	c. Ask him who he knows.		

If I choose this action:	Then I might value this:	Other evidence in my life:

4. Which do you want most out of life?

   a. Financial success.
   b. Fulfilling career.
   c. Loving family and friends.

5. How would you spend $15,000 if you won it in a contest?

   a. Start a business.
   b. Quit your job or school.
   c. Put it in a bank.

6. If you could do as you wished for a day, what would you do?

   a. Go on a shopping spree.
   b. Fly to a faraway, fascinating place.
   c. Spend time with a special friend.

7. If your supervisor asked you to "fudge" a little on orders, what would you do?

   a. Do what she/he said.
   b. Openly refuse.
   c. Ignore the suggestion and keep quiet.

8. If you were asked to participate in a college program which provided extra tutoring and counseling, what would you do?

    a. Gladly accept.
    b. Refuse because you did not need it.
    c. Refuse because of the time needed.
    d. Accept but plan to drop if you did not like it.

Discuss your answers to the preceding questions with others in your class. As you do so, concentrate on the following questions.

a. Does a particular choice seem to suggest several different values? Which choices?

b. What was the hardest aspect of this exercise?

c. Why was it difficult?

How much of the time do you think your decisions about risks are based on your values? Discuss your answer.

Think About Values

How did you use Thinking Tools to sort out your memories of past actions and find the **values** they represented?

Exercise 7h

Risk-Taking In College

College is full of risks. It is different from high school in many ways, and often students have to change their lifestyles in order to succeed. Here are two people who must decide whether or not to risk changing their ways. Help them.

1. Every campus has a Mr. Cool, and Trent State is no exception. Eli is well-known on campus even as a freshman as the best dresser, best dancer, and smoothest talker. He takes academics lightly and extracurricular activities heavily. He strolls into classes late, falls asleep regularly, seldom participates in discussions, and rarely does homework assignments.

   Eli thinks it is cool to be "laid back" about school. After all, it got him through high school — teachers would not dare to fail such a cool person! Unfortunately, he has not been able to sweet talk a few college instructors, and now he is failing in three courses.

   The counselor has worked with Eli on several occasions. They have discussed the types of study strategies, behaviors and attitudes that successful students employ. Eli recognizes the differences between what he does and what his counselor suggests. He can even identify students he knows who use those other strategies. Some of them are people he looked down on in high school who are now getting much better grades than he is.

   Eli is reluctant. What would the other students think? Would they think he was a wimp? Could he be partly cool and partly a serious student? And what if he volunteered to answer a question and then missed it? Eli is suddenly confused and afraid.

a. What would Eli do if he used a pessimistic risk-taking strategy?

b. What would he do with a safe risk-taking strategy?

c. What would he do with an optimistic risk-taking strategy?

d. What are the possibilities that something bad will happen if he continues his current study habits?

What bad thing might happen?

e. What are the possibilities that a good thing might happen if he changes his study patterns?

What good thing(s)?

f. List all the things that you think Eli values in this situation.

g. Which of Eli's values are in conflict?

h. What would you do in this situation? Why?

i. Discuss your answers with your team or the class.

2. When his trigonometry instructor told the class that they would need a special programmable calculator, Rob panicked. He had no money, no job, and his folks were stretched out just paying for his tuition, books and other college expenses. He could not afford a calculator, and he could not stand the idea of failing the class — and maybe college — because he did not have one. Rob had never failed a class and did not want to start now. He very much wanted a college degree so he could help himself and his parents.

   Depressed, Rob went to the bookstore just to see how much the calculator cost. The shop was crowded with students buying and returning books; new shipments were being brought in at the same time. Rob suddenly wondered if he could slip the small calculator into his jacket and walk out. Chances were that no one would notice because they were so busy.

   Rob could see one clerk behind the counter and another busy receiving a new shipment of books. There seemed to be no other clerks in the store. He did not think that the store had a beeper system like the library's, which buzzed when someone walked out with books. He did not see anyone who looked like a faculty member or a guard.

   Rob thought he could walk out with a calculator and get away with it even though he had never stolen so much as a toothpick before. He also realized it was going to get even more hectic in the bookstore in a half hour when noon classes got out.

   a. What would Rob do with a:

      1. Safe risk-taking strategy?

      2. Optimistic risk-taking strategy?

3. Pessimistic risk-taking strategy?

b. List at least six pieces of relevant information that Rob has available in this situation. For each piece of information, indicate if it is: reliable (R), somewhat reliable (SR), or not reliable (NR).

1.

2.

3.

4.

5.

6.

7.

c. What does Rob value in this situation? With your team, list three things he values and, for each one, state what he would do in the situation if he valued that the most.

1. He values:

   If he valued it most, then he would:

2. He values:

   If he valued it most, then he would:

3. He values:

   If he valued it most, then he would:

d. What would you do in this situation?

e. Why? After answering, discuss your answer with others.

Exercise 7i

Finding Your Own Risk-Taking Tendencies

The only way you can get a good idea of the type of risk-taker you really are is to think about choices you have actually made. In the space below describe the toughest decision you have had to make in the past two or three years. Describe the situation. List the alternatives you had. Explain the implications of those alternatives. Then answer the questions at the end.

Decision:

Situation:

Choices and implications:

1. What did you decide?

2. What kind of risk-taking strategy was that?

3. What values were involved?

4. What did you finally value the most in your choice?

5. How reliable was your information?

6. Based on those answers and all the other answers in this chapter, what kind of risk-taker do you think you usually are?

Exercise 7j

Thinking Tools With Risk-Taking

Risk-taking is one of the more clear-cut mental activities we undertake. Very often we know that we are weighing the risks before doing something. It is often a more conscious activity than thinking about cause-and-effect or finding patterns. This makes Thinking Tools an important aspect of risk-taking.

> In the last exercise you recalled and analyzed a risk-taking situation you had experienced. Put yourself back in that situation again. Think about what was happening.

Below, list the four most powerful Thinking Tools that you recall using and then explain how you used each one.

1. Thinking Tool:

   Use:

2. Thinking Tool:

   Use:

3. Thinking Tool:

   Use:

4. Thinking Tool:

   Use:

Describe the risk-taking situation to someone else in your class. Describe the Thinking Tools you believe you used. See if he or she can suggest other Thinking Tools that you might have been using in that situation. List any others here:

Supplemental Exercise 7k

Risking A College Choice

Cathy is about to graduate from high school. She is trying to decide what college to attend next year and what to study. Her parents are not wealthy, and she would probably have to work part-time if she went to Pate Community College. Pate has very little scholarship money to offer, but it does not cost too much, anyway. It offers the kinds of hi-tech programs Cathy thinks she might want to study, but she fears that a two-year program might not prepare her for top-level jobs in computers, robotics, lasers.

McKinney College, on the other hand, could give her a scholarship. However, McKinney mainly offers degrees in social science and art, areas in which Cathy is not particularly interested. McKinney does have a fairly good business program which might be a possibility.

Polk University also has excellent programs in computers and robotics. But Polk is expensive and difficult; Cathy is not sure she could make it easily. Her advisor says it might take longer for Cathy to finish Polk because she might have to take a lighter load and work part-time to afford the tuition.

Cathy's real dream has always been to attend Rainey University, which has an excellent academic reputation. It attracts the best students and its graduates get very good jobs. It might be possible to get a scholarship; Rainey sets aside money for minorities (Cathy is black). But Rainey is very hard and Cathy has only been a B+ student in high school. She is not sure she could make it. Also, Rainey does not have high-tech majors. The closest thing is an automated business program.

Cathy's parents are willing to make whatever sacrifice they can for her, but Cathy does not want to be a burden on them. She wants very much to be a big job success. Above all, she does not want to embarrass her parents or herself by failing in what she does.

1. Cathy has four choices of colleges. Rate each one (1-4, with 1 being most risky) in terms of the risks of going there. For the top two (1 and 2), also explain what the risk is.

   ____ a. Polk University

   ____ b. Pate Community College

   ____ c. Rainey University

   ____ d. McKinney College

2. What college would you pick with each risk-taking strategy? Explain why.
   a. Pessimistic strategy?

   b. Safe strategy?

   c. Optimistic strategy?

3. Which college would you pick in this situation?

4. Why?

Supplemental Exercise 7L

What Would You Do?

Below are listed four choice situations, each with some alternatives. Pick the choice you would make for each situation by putting an "X" in the proper space.

1. If you had $5,000 to invest, what would you do?

    ____ Put it in a bank at 10 percent interest (earning $500 a year).

    ____ Buy low-risk stocks that could yield about $2,000 a year profit with a 30 percent chance of losing all of your money.

    ____ Buy high-risk stocks which might triple your money in a year with a 55 percent chance of losing all of your money.

Why did you choose that particular investment?

2. You are a football coach, and your team has just scored a touchdown. The score is 13-14 against you with 47 seconds left in the game. If you run or pass for the extra point and make it, you get 2 more points and win, 15-14. If you kick for the extra point and make it, you get one more point and tie the game 14-14. If you miss any type of extra point (pass, run or kick), you get no more points and lose the game 13-14. The team you are playing is your traditional rival. Which do you choose?

____ To kick the extra point, with a 75 percent chance of making it.

____ To run for the extra point. You have the best running team in the league, but your opponent has the second best defense against the run.

____ To pass for the extra point. Your passing game is not very good, but your opponent has the second worst defense against the pass.

Why did you choose this strategy?

3. Which of these would you choose?

____ A job that offers a 30 percent chance of a very large income, excellent advancement but a 70 percent chance of losing the job.

____ A job that offers a 60 percent chance of a good income, not much chance of advancement and a 40 percent chance of losing the job.

____ A job with a small immediate income, a 50 percent chance of advancement and a 50 percent chance of losing the job.

____ None of these, but wait for something better to come along. In this case, describe below what you mean by "better".

Why did you choose this particular job?

4. You need a scholarship to attend college. You may be offered one for $2,000 from the college you really want to attend, but you will not know for another month. You have just been offered a $900 scholarship from another college, and you must tell them *yes* or *no* within a week. What do you do?

   ____ Accept the $900 scholarship from the first college.

   ____ Turn that scholarship down and hope the larger one is offered to you.

Why did you make this particular choice?

Is there any other choice that you can think of? If so, what is it?

5. What risk-taking strategy did you use in numbers 1-4?
   Number 1:

   Number 2:

   Number 3:

   Number 4:

6. What did you value most in each choice you made above?
   In #1, I valued:

   In #2, I valued:

   In #3, I valued:

   In #4, I valued:

7. What kind of risk-taker do you think you are, based on your answers on the previous page?

Explain why you think you are that type of risk-taker.

Think About It!

What Thinking Tools did you use to make a decision in the third activity? Be specific.

Chapter Eight

Organizing Information

We instinctively group and label information to bring order out of chaos. As effective thinkers learn more, however, they are ready to scrap these tentative labels.

Classifying information is one of the most common mental activities — and one of the most complicated. To **classify**, you need to think in many different ways at the same time. You need to juggle possibilities. You need to use all of the skills from previous chapters: relevance, cause-and-effect, testing possibilities, and you need new skills, too. It becomes very complicated.

The difficulties with organizing information begin with the fact that there is no one right way to do it. We instinctively group and label information to bring some type of order out of chaos. But for effective thinkers, first labels are always tentative; such people are ready to change or scrap labels as they learn more.

We can organize any given set of information in many ways. For instance, think about all of the items in your pockets or purse. You can group them by colors, shape, size, weight, or by purpose. Any of these classifications might be useful in organizing, depending on your purpose.

This chapter includes three fundamental skills you must have before you can organize information effectively. As usual, you may already have those skills to a degree. If so, become aware of them and practice them.

If not, learn them. The three skills, stated as objectives, are as follows:

- You will be able to label or categorize groups of information based on the characteristics of the information.
- You will be able to imagine several ways to organize the information available about a given situation.
- You will be able to sort lists of information into useful groups.

Since you can usually group information in several ways, how do you know which way is best? There is no certain answer to that question. In general the best sets of categories have (at least) the following four characteristics:

a. The categories will be **useful** — they will fit the information and the situation.

b. The categories will be **inclusive** — they will be large enough to hold all (or almost all) of the useful information.

c. The categories will **discriminate** — they will clearly show the differences that matter in the situation.

d. The categories will be **accurate** — they will use the information as it actually is rather than twisting it to make it fit.

When you obtain information or find yourself in a certain situation, you need to do several things. You need to sort the information into trial groups and then see if the groups meet the four characteristics above. If they do, you have good groups for that situation. If they do not, then you need to experiment by changing the groups and finding other possibilities which fit better. You need to label the categories. And, often, as you start, you need to imagine possible groups and try them out.

What is an example of a good set of categories? A restaurant menu is a fine example. It divides your choices into such categories as meats, vegetables, salads, beverages. Those categories are useful — they help you find things easily. They are inclusive — all the choices fit into them. They discriminate — steak versus rice versus peas. And they are accurate — unless the restaurant is out of something, which is not the fault of the categories.

Exercise 8a

Organizing Labels

Think about the following statements we hear every day.

"That was a good idea."

"He is a nice guy."

"I've had a horrible day."

Consciously or unconsciously, we label or categorize events, feelings, ideas, people. Have you ever been to a party and met many new people? Or encountered many people during your first days at college? What were you thinking about as you met, talked to, or observed them? You were probably labeling them. You met them, and you neatly filed them in different ways: macho, chic, dumb, sharp, well-dressed, ugly, caring, sexy, cute, snobbish.

Our first label for a person is a hypothesis — a tentative assumption about the person. We label him or her in order to find a place for the person in our mental scheme of things, but we are really not sure if that is where that person fits. Our label is temporary, and we wait to see if it is appropriate, or if we need to change the label later.

As we get to know somebody, we often change our label. We change our hypothesis as we see the person differently, more fully. Next time you go to a mall, shopping center or public event, think about it. Observe the people and think about how you label them.

We label information in the same way. We take it in and then put it into tentative file boxes. We make a guess as to where it fits in our data base. For effective thinkers, such labels are tentative at first. Effective thinkers consider other possible labels, find more information, change their labeling system. Labeling is the difference between confusion and order, misunderstanding and understanding, whether you are labeling people or information. It is our way of putting new things into a mental file drawer.

The three activities in this exercise help you to become more conscious of the labeling skills which you probably already have and use. They take you through three stages: identify labels when given several choices; select the most general term (label) from a group; and generate labels that fit several items.

1. Below you are given several items of specific information followed by several general labels or categories. Study the choices listed and then circle the best label for each group of items. Remember the four characteristics of good organization listed in the Introduction to this chapter.

Note: *You may not recognize all of the names in some groups. If not, look them up.*

Choices:

a. Edgar Allen Poe
b. Henry Wadsworth Longfellow
c. Alfred, Lord Tennyson
d. Elizabeth Barrett Browning

The best label is (circle one):

1. Poets
2. Writers
3. Famous people
4. Novelists

Choices:

a. Baptist
b. Methodist
c. Presbyterian
d. Lutheran

The best label is (circle one):

1. Churches
2. Protestant religions
3. Religions
4. Proper nouns

Choices:

a. George Washington
b. Robert E. Lee
c. Dwight Eisenhower
d. George Patton

The best label is (circle one):

1. Famous men
2. Presidents
3. American generals
4. Americans

Choices:

a. 3
b. .176
c. 17 + 4
d. x + 2
e. 221 · 312

The best label is (circle one):

1. Measures
2. Numbers
3. Formulas
4. Symbols

Choices:

a. Governor
b. Mayor
c. President
d. Senator
e. Councilman

The best label is (circle one):

1. Candidates
2. Politicians
3. Public Figures
4. Speakers

Share your answers with your team or the class and discuss them.

2. In each group below, there are several ideas or topics given. Some are specific, some are general —they fit all the members of the group. Your job is to circle the letter of the most general item in the group. Then explain why that is the most general item in the group. One example is given.

Example:

a. Fir
b. Pine
c. Cedar
(d.) Evergreen

Answer: Evergreen (circle "d" above).

Reasons: All are trees. All are green most or all of the year. Therefore, they must be a type of evergreen tree.

A. a. Navy
   b. Army
   c. Coast Guard
   d. Armed Forces
   e. Marines

Reasons:

B. a. Manic depression
   b. Paranoia
   c. Schizophrenia
   d. Psychosis

Reasons:

C. a. Sun
   b. Asteroids
   c. Solar system
   d. Meteors
   e. Comets
   f. Planets

Reasons:

D. a. Must be approved by simple majority vote.
   b. May be introduced in either House.
   c. Must be approved by the other House.
   d. Passing of a bill.
   e. Approved or vetoed by the President.

Reasons:

E. a. A pioneer home.
   b. Education and religion.
   c. A pioneer settlement.
   d. Social activities.
   e. Indian attacks.
   f. Law and order.

Reasons:

F. a. Water movement.
   b. Photosynthesis.
   c. Germination.
   d. Respiration.
   e. How plants grow.

Reasons:

G. a. Alaska
   b. North America
   c. Mexico
   d. Washington
   e. Canada

Reasons:

H. a. Physiology
   b. Science
   c. Biology
   d. Chemistry
   e. Anatomy

Reasons:

I. a. Clavicle
b. Pelvis
c. Tibia
d. Humerus
e. Bones

Reasons:

J. a. Emerald
b. Gems
c. Rubies
d. Sapphires
e. Opals

Reasons:

What did you do to identify the most general item in those groups? Think back to your mental activity when you wrestled with those items. What techniques did you use?

Share your answers with your team, and try to come up with a larger list of mental techniques that you used in this activity.

3. In this labeling activity, you do not have a list from which to choose. You have several items of information — topics, facts, names. Your task is to determine the organizing category by yourself. Decide what to label each group of items and write the label above the group. Use the four characteristics of good categories. Find a label that is as accurate and specific as possible. Try to avoid very general labels.

   A. Label: ______________________________

      a. Situation comedy
      b. Soap operas
      c. Games
      d. Variety
      e. News
      f. Dramatic series

   B. Label: ______________________________

      a. Preface
      b. Table of contents
      c. Index
      d. Appendix
      e. Title page
      f. Copyright

   C. Label: ______________________________

      a. Offsides
      b. Illegal motion
      c. Holding
      d. Clipping
      e. Interference

   D. Label: ______________________________

      a. Nouns
      b. Verbs
      c. Adjectives
      d. Adverbs
      e. Pronouns

E. Label: ______________________________

a. $\frac{x}{y}$

b. $\frac{5}{8}$

c. $\frac{32}{63}$

d. $\frac{x - y}{z}$

F. Label: ______________________________

a. Bahamas
b. Sandwich
c. Oahu
d. Madagascar
e. Falkland

G. Label: ______________________________

a. Drought
b. Fog
c. Flood
d. Avalanche

H. Label: ______________________________

a. Income
b. Property
c. Inheritance
d. Sales
e. Excise

I. Label: ______________________________

a. 1.79 cc
b. .75 pounds
c. 32 meters
d. 2.9 tons
e. .13 miles

J. Label: ______________________________

a. $5 = 7 - 2$
b. $2x + 7 = 19y$
c. $L \times W = A$
d. $D = 2R$
e. $77 - 33 + 2 = 46$

Share your answers with others in your class. Discuss them and change any answers you wish to, based on that discussion. Then as a team answer this question:

Think About It!

How did you know what the **overall categories** were in these situations?

Exercise 8b

Figuring Possible Categories In The Real World

People are sorters. When we face a situation that has many parts or much information, we naturally try to sort it out. We also begin by imagining all the ways in which we can sort it out. Let's say you make a list of groceries to buy. You probably would not just scramble the list. You probably would sort it out in some way.

How might you sort a grocery list? A dietician might sort it by food groups — dairy products, green vegetables. An especially organized person might list it under each aisle number. Most of us would do something — for example, we might organize the list by general parts of the store. We would then know where to look on the list when in a certain part of the store. We would sort out our items in a way most useful to us.

In this exercise imagine you are faced with a lot of information and must sort it out. You must first imagine all the possible ways you could sort it out — only then would you be ready to pick the best method. Here are several situations. For each one, list as many possible ways to sort the information as you can.

1. You are skimming a group of recipes in a newspaper or a new cookbook. How many ways do you naturally think of to sort those recipes? For example, you might rate them by ease of preparation — which ones are easiest and which are hardest. List some other ways of sorting recipes below.

2. You are entering college and have to choose between many different programs of study — electronics, history, computers, business, art. Your mind naturally imagines many ways to organize the information, such as by the program's reputation for being easy or difficult. Below, list some other ways you might sort out all that information.

3. Circle one of the three situations below and identify as many possible ways as you can to organize the information.

   a. You have collected much information for a research paper on the history of your neighborhood. Your instructor asks you to organize it in several different ways.

      or

   b. You have collected 2,000 baseball cards and want to organize them. What are your alternatives?

      or

   c. You are hired to set up a new system for filing case histories of welfare clients. What ways might you set them up?

Share your answers with the class or with your team. As you do so, discuss the possible organizing methods in terms of this question:

When would that organizing method be useful?

Exercise 8c

Organizing Subgroups Within Main Groups

As you have seen, it is fairly easy to identify several different ways to group most information. This, however, is only the start of organizing information. The next step is to decide how to divide the information within the group you have chosen. How many sub-groups do you need and which ones make the most sense? Imagine you are organizing people and have decided to group them by their age. That would be the first step.

The next step would be to decide how to break down the list further. Sometimes it would make sense to subdivide age by each year (1, 2, 3, and so on). Sometimes it would make sense to divide people into only two age groups (voting age or not). More often, it would be most useful to break the group into several sub-groups:

0-17   18-24   25-34   35-48   49-64   65-up

How would you decide that those were the best sub-groups? By looking at your purposes or the information you had. As usual, **best** means most useful in that situation.

Below are listed some people on a politician's list of potential voters. Read the information; then organize it in the ways asked.

Jerome Davis — 32; architect; black; married; 2 children; $65,000 annual income; college graduate; lives on north side of town; staunch Republican.

Harold Inabinet — 49; truck driver; white; divorced; $37,000 annual income; two years college; lives on the east side of town; votes Democratic.

Mary Jordan	—	housewife; widowed; 1 child; 29 years old; $13,500 annual income from life insurance; not a registered voter; high school graduate; lives in town.
L. B. Jacques	—	phone company lineman; lives east of town; usually a Democratic voter; $32,000 combined income; no children; married; college graduate; 35; white.
Robert Keck	—	black; $16,200 income; 57; baker; 1 child; 10th grade education; lives in town; newly registered voter.
Eppie Pandiscio	—	teacher; unmarried; Master's degree; Republican; $21,350 annual salary; black; lives in the north side of town; no children; 51.
R. F. Ramos	—	35; married; policeman; community college graduate; $19,400 annual income; lives east of town; 2 children; Independent voter; Spanish-American.
Julia Rabinowitz	—	unemployed; 25 years old; married; no permanent address; $5,675 income (welfare); registered, but never votes; no children; white; high school graduate.
K.V. Pow	—	47; lives north of town; $72,000 annual income; medical school graduate; oriental; divorced; Republican; doctor.
Poteet Preece	—	black; 33; $16,250 annual income; lives west of town; registered Democrat; minister; 5 children; widowed; college graduate.
Connie Coleman	—	21; $7,200 income; student; lives at college in town; new voter; white; unmarried.

1. As a team, organize these people according to their financial status. First create sub-groups; then list the people who fall into each sub-group.

Explain why you selected those sub-groups; what use will they be to a politician?

Think About Groups!

What Thinking Tools did you use to decide which **subcategories** made sense and were useful?

2. Now organize the political list another way. This time create sub-groups in terms of education and list the names within each. Do that in the space below.

3. As a class suggest as many other ways to divide up that list of potential voters as you can.

4. Divide into teams, each team taking one of those new ways of dividing the list. Each team should create sub-groups within the overall method on a separate page. When your team is finished, compare sub-groups with the other teams.

Exercise 8d

Organizing Jobs Into Groups

Jobs fall into groups in terms of such things as duties, educational requirements, salary, status. Below are listed twenty jobs. We will consider various ways to group them depending on what you want to do with the groups.

a. Machinist
b. Doctor
c. Mayor
d. Plumber
e. Biologist
f. Judge
g. Janitor
h. Lawyer
i. Bus Driver
j. Assembly Line Worker
k. Mathematician
l. Architect
m. Waiter
n. County Commissioner
o. Dentist
p. Biochemist
q. Carpenter
r. Deputy Sheriff
s. Telephone Operator
t. Astronomer

1. Organize those jobs in terms of functional categories. For example, you might place a coach, professional golfer and sports writer in a category called sports people. The rules for this exercise are: create four or five categories; label each category; and fit three to six jobs into each category. List your categories and the related jobs in the space below.

2. Compare your categories and assignments with others in the class. Discuss any differences and try to figure out **why** you differed. Write your reasons here.

3. Now choose one other way to organize those twenty jobs, such as by education required, salary, or work with things/ideas/people. Do not choose to organize them alphabetically (that is too easy). Figure out subcategories within this new organizational scheme; then put the jobs into those subcategories just as you did at the start of this exercise.

Think About Organizing Jobs

Think carefully about how you tried out **alternatives** in this exercise. How did you use your Thinking Tools?

Exercise 8e

Grouping Life Experiences

Elinor is a professional writer. Manuel, her friend, comes to her for help. He has just graduated from Bumpo College and is starting to look for a job. He has had some work experience but not much. Elinor talks to Manuel and writes down all the things he tells her about himself. She then asks him to go home, think about the list, and organize the items on it into groups. Below are the items she wrote down about Manuel.

a. 24 years old.
b. Graduate of Bumpo College.
c. Member of St. Mark's church.
d. Unmarried.
e. Lifeguard at Bumpo College pool, summer of 1983.
f. President of Newman Club at Bumpo.
g. Member of the track team.
h. College work-study at Bumpo business office, 1983-84.
i. Salesman for McBrides Department Store, summer of 1984.
j. Graduated with a psychology major.
k. Graduated in the top 15 percent of his high school class.
l. One of his hobbies is programming microcomputers.
m. Has a strong letter of recommendation from the psychology department chairman.
n. Had a 3.47 GPA from Bumpo.
o. Likes to write.
p. Not sure of his career goal.
q. Colorblind.
r. Willing to move if the job is right.
s. Part-time job as scheduling assistant at the Gadsden Trucking Company, 1980-83.
t. Father is a lawyer; mother is a businesswoman.
u. Excellent health.
v. No steady girlfriend.

1. Organize Manuel's list of items into three or four related groups in the space below. Be sure to give each group a label.

   a.

   b.

   c.

   d.

   Discuss your categories and items with your team or the entire class. Explain your way of organizing the information if they do not understand it.

2. Elinor and Manuel now sit down with their categories. Elinor explains that Manuel needs a resume: a list showing his accomplishments, experience, background. A resume will tell an employer who Manuel is and why he should be hired. Manuel has the grouped information for the resume and now must put it in a logical and appealing order. Put the categories in the order you think would be best for Manuel's resume.

   First category would be:

   Next category would be:

   Next category would be:

   Next category would be:

   Discuss the order of your categories with others, listen to their ideas and revise your order of categories if needed.

3. Elinor says that the third step in resume writing is to decide on the titles of the categories. You gave each category a descriptive title in the first activity. Is it a short title? In a resume, each category needs a one-to-three word title. If yours are not that short, find shorter titles that are still appropriate.

   The first category's title is:

   The next category's title is:

   The next category's title is:

   The next category's title is:

4. The final step, Elinor tells Manuel, is to check for missing information. Is there other information that Manuel should give employers on his resume? If so, list the types of missing information below; you can make up information if you wish. Show where such information should be placed in the resume. Do this as a team.

5. Outline your own resume on a separate sheet using these steps. When you decide to look for a job you will need to update it and make copies.

Exercise 8f

Organizing Research Notes

Jan must write a research paper for her English class. She has decided to write the paper on leukemia. If Jan had been thinking, she would have done some organizing and planning first. Instead, she quickly read some articles and made a lot of notes. Now Jan has many notecards with information on them. She does not know when to quit collecting information and start writing. She does not know how to organize her information. Because it is all on different cards, she is not even sure what information she has. Below is a list of the headings on those note cards.

a. Leads to anemia.
b. A kind of cancer.
c. Exact causes unclear.
d. Can cause enlarged spleen.
e. Blood transfusion used in treatment.
f. Chronic leukemia.
g. Patient may bleed easily.
h. Enlarged lymph glands may occur.
i. Possibly caused by chemicals.
j. Acute leukemia.
k. Radiation therapy to relieve symptoms.
l. Large doses of radiation may contribute to cause.
m. May recur after treatment.
n. May be caused by a genetic disorder.
o. Harm from uncontrolled growth of white blood cells.
p. Blood production in bone marrow affected.
q. Leucocytes — white blood cells — uncontrolled growth.
r. Function of white blood cells.
s. Other types of cancer.

Jan needs to get organized. Particularly, she needs to organize her information into an outline containing no more than four or five major parts. Can you do it? Group the items, label the groups, and indicate which pieces of information (by letter) you would put under that heading.

I.

II.

III.

IV.

V.

1. Which parts of her information could Jan leave out of her paper? List the letters (if any) below.

2. What additional information should Jan include in her report? List at least three areas in which Jan should do additional research.

3. How would organizing information help with the following research paper tasks?

   a. Gathering information.

   b. Deciding what to cover.

   c. Sifting out the information you collect.

d. Figuring out the flow of the paper.

e. Actually writing the paper.

4. Discuss with your team how you actually prepare research papers. Identify differences in approach among the team members. Below list any techniques you hear which seem helpful and which you want to think about using when you write papers.

5. With the class, discuss this question:
What is the best way to prepare research papers?

Exercise 8g

Organizing Questions By Difficulty Level

Which of these questions seems harder?

- Who was commander of the Union forces at the end of the American Civil War?

- What influences has the American Civil War had on political behavior in the South during the 20th century?

If you do not know either answer both questions might seem hard. But you probably decided that the second question was harder. Why? The first one needs only a single definite answer — a name (Ulysses S. Grant). The answer to the second question demands extensive ideas and information arranged to show the relationships among history, economics, politics. The answer to question two requires much more information.

Different questions require different types and amounts of thought. On tests they also demonstrate different degrees of learning. You have surely noticed that some kinds of questions are harder, some easier. That is because their answers require different types and amounts of learning and of thinking. The simplest questions only ask you to remember a certain fact. The hardest ones ask you to remember facts and to show the relationships among them.

1. Below are listed some psychology test questions. As a team put them into three groups according to how difficult that question is to answer. Do not worry about whether or not you know the answer; evaluate the type of question.

    a. Define the term "psychology".

    b. Evaluate the contribution of psychology to social problems.

    c. Give examples of applying psychology to social problems.

    d. Illustrate the psychological process of "shaping".

    e. Contrast independent and dependent variables in an experiment.

    f. Identify William Wundt.

    g. Explore the implications of Pavlov's experiment with classical conditioning for American education.

    h. Of the early psychologists (such as Skinner, Piaget, James, Watson), which one contributed the most to the study of psychology as it is today? Explain why.

    i. Interpret the graph on page 44 by explaining the general trend demonstrated.

    j. The learning of complicated tasks through operant conditioning is called "chunking". True or false?

    k. How could operant conditioning help relieve psychosomatic illnesses?

    l. Outline the history of psychology in the 19th and 20th centuries.

    m. Give two original examples of operant behavior.

n. Distinguish between these techniques for studying behavior: the experiment, naturalistic observation, tests, interviews, questionnaires.

o. Why is reinforcement a key to learning?

p. List the three kinds of systems of memory.

q. Illustrate a mnemonic device.

r. What is "chunking"?

Group the test questions by placing their letters below these categories.

Harder	Medium	Easier

2. Why are the questions hard or easy? What is there about the questions that makes them harder or easier? Give each of the three groups a more descriptive label, one that talks about the quality of the questions.

   Harder questions are those that:

   Medium questions are those that:

   Easier questions are those that:

3. As a team answer the following questions.

   a. What are the best ways to study for the first type of test question?

   b. What are the best ways to study for the second type of test question?

   c. What are the best ways to study for the third type of test question?

Homework

During the next two weeks, collect any tests or quizzes you take. Classify the test questions in terms of these three groups. Copy them on three separate pages (one for each category). Make a fourth sheet for those questions that do not seem to fit into any of the three categories. After two weeks bring the sheets to class and share them.

Exercise 8h

Using Thinking Tools When Organizing

Organizing information is a complicated mental activity. Your mind has to do many things at one time or in sequence. You must imagine and then test alternate possibilities. You must systematically lump items together. You cannot excel at organizing information unless you have already mastered many of the thinking skills from previous chapters. In short, to organize information well you must be knowledgeable, creative and orderly. It is something like leading a mental orchestra. No wonder some people do not like to do it!

As your mental activities become more complicated, your uses of Thinking Tools also become more complicated — and more important. When a woodworker builds a cabinet, she or he must apply many different skills at the same time to do the best job: cutting, measuring, smoothing, gluing, designing, fitting. You, as a thinker, must use many mental skills when you practice the basics of organizing information.

Your toolkit must be well packed. You need to be sure you have all the right Thinking Tools in the kit to handle the demands. Go back over this chapter carefully and then fill in the box.

My Thinking Toolkit contains the following tools for the basics of **organizing information**:

Supplemental Exercise 8i

Sorting Out Information About A New Class

We sort information all the time; it is part of being human. Think about entering a class for the first time. You absorb all sorts of information about that class — what it will be like and what it might mean for you.

How you organize that information depends on you. You bring your own set of categories with you. You might sort it this way: *positive towards this class* (P), *negative towards this class* (N), and *not sure* (?). Below are some things you might notice about a new class. Sort them by putting P, N or ? before each one. Write the first answer which occurs to you.

____ a. The classroom has a big window.

____ b. I see one of my good friends sitting there.

____ c. The classroom has an overhead projector set up.

____ d. All the seats at the very back are already taken.

____ e. The instructor is wearing a sports shirt and slacks.

____ f. The lights in this classroom seem dim.

____ g. Everyone seems to have their books, and I haven't bought mine yet.

____ h. The instructor is staring at us with no expression.

___ i. The room seats about 60 people and is filling up rapidly.

____ j. I see two people in the class that are real cut-ups; I don't like them.

____ k. The room seems chilly.

____ l. The instructor looks like he is in his 50s.

____ m. The instructor has written the name of the course on the board, and he wrote very slowly.

____ n. The seats are hard, small, and close together.

____ o. There is a flower in a vase on the desk.

____ p. There is also a bunch of papers on the desk; they look like handouts.

____ q. After ten minutes in the course, the instructor is already lecturing.

____ r. I am sitting between a pretty girl and a nice-looking guy.

____ s. The instructor has handed out a list of course objectives and a page about how we will be graded.

____ t. I am sitting in front and about as far from the door as I can get.

____ u. The instructor has a smooth voice.

Below, put the items of information (by letters) under the three groups.

Positive	Negative	Not Sure

Share your answers with others — your team or the entire class. When there are disagreements, explain your reasons for putting the items where you did. Remember there are no right answers to these — your grouping reflects your values, priorities, needs.

As a class, see if you can list at least five other things you might notice when you enter a new class. Indicate whether they are positive, negative, or if you are not sure.

As a class identify and discuss any items on the list which a student might tend to rate one way and an instructor might tend to rate another way. For example, a student might rate item *t* as negative, while the instructor might rate it as positive, interpreting it as a sign that the student is interested in learning. Discuss why they might differ.

Think About Different Perspectives

How do you employ Thinking Tools when you are trying to decide on **differences** between student and instructor viewpoints?

Supplemental Exercise 8j

Imagining The Advertising Possibilities

Sherman has recently graduated from Ogilvie State College and taken a job with an advertising agency. His first assignment is to work with an advertising pro to market the CRAM vitamin.

What is CRAM? It is a new vitamin product. The people who manufacture CRAM claim it increases learning ability, memory and recall when taken twice a day. They say that poor students become excellent ones after they take CRAM; good students become outstanding ones after using CRAM. After using CRAM, students can learn difficult material in less time and remember it longer.

The advertising pro asks Sherman to come up with a list of possible buyers for this product. He says this is the first step in advertising. Only then is it possible to plan the full advertising campaign that will sell those particular buyers on CRAM.

1. Below, write all of the possible types of buyers that Sherman might list. Two examples are given.

   a. College counselors

   b. Trainers for the U.S. Air Force

   c.

   d.

   e.

   f.

2. Select six of the buyers you have listed. Figure out how Sherman could appeal to each group in order to convince them to buy CRAM vitamins: what arguments would influence them? List your answers below. One example is given.

   - College counselors. Convince them to buy CRAM vitamins and give them to all of the students on academic probation so the students will learn more, pass the tests, and no longer be on academic probation.

   a.

   b.

   c.

   d.

   e.

   f.

3. Name three other jobs or career areas where imagining possible ways of sorting information would be especially important.

   -
   -
   -

Chapter Nine

Classification Charts

There is no one right way to organize. We need to first figure out what we want to do, then make the information serve that purpose. We must be the master; the information, the servant.

Organizing information usefully is difficult because we must keep many pieces of information in mind at the same time. It is similar to juggling seven or eight balls at once; the juggler often drops some balls. When making choices involving considerable amounts of information, we often forget items and must start over. We may even be half-paralyzed by the fear of forgetting something important.

Why does this happen? Because our minds are what researchers call **limited capacity information processors.** What that means is that each of us has a very limited amount of brainpower to use actively and consciously at any given moment. It is comparable to having only a small table to use in spreading out many pieces of paper. Once the table is covered, we cannot add more paper without covering something that is already on the table.

Too often, people use all of that available mental space in simply trying to keep track of the information. They have no brainpower left over to actually do anything with the information. They spend enormous amounts of mental energy trying to make certain they have not dropped any key information out of their active memory, but unfortunately they seldom make much progress towards a solution. They are very inefficient thinkers.

One secret of efficient thinking with our limited capacity information processors is organization. Collecting information helps a lot, as you know. Grouping information usefully helps even more. In complicated situations, the action which helps most is to group the information usefully **on paper**.

If the information is grouped usefully on paper you no longer have to expend your mental energy keeping track of it in your active mind. You can refer to the paper in order to find specific information. This allows you to use your available mental powers to think of alternatives, consequences, patterns, hypotheses.

This chapter explores one method of organizing information usefully on paper: a classification chart. A classification chart is only one of many possible techniques for organizing complex sets of information. As you go through college, you will probably learn other ways. In the next few exercises you will explore classification charts by accomplishing two key objectives:

1. To be able to draw and fill in a classification chart.

2. To be able to extract the key parts of a classification chart from complex personal, job, and academic situations.

A classification chart is a way to compare your alternative choices with your information categories. It helps make clear how the information relates to your choices. It lists your choices down the left side, and your categories of information across the top. Boxes called *cells* are formed where the lines cross.

A classification chart looks like this:

Choices	Information Category 1	Information Category 2	Information Category 3	Information Category 4
Choice #1				
Choice #2				
Choice #3				
Choice #4				

To make such a classification chart, you must make a series of decisions: what alternatives you wish to consider, what types of information you find relevant to those alternatives, and what specific pieces of information you have or want. Often we make these decisions while we are constructing the classification chart.

Imagine you are thinking about buying a car. You have the following information about three cars that interest you:

- Cadillac — has an excellent ride,disk brakes, costs $16,950, looks very impressive.
- Chevrolet — costs $10,200, has fair looks, gets 27 miles per gallon, has a good ride but doesn't have disk brakes.
- Toyota — gets 38 miles per gallon, has disk brakes, costs $7,500, looks okay, has a bumpy ride.
- Ford — has disk brakes, costs $7,950, looks sleek, gets 35 miles per gallon, has a fair ride.

Which car is right for you based on this information (and, of course, other information and opinions that you personally have)? It is easier to answer that question if you put all of the information in a classification chart. How? Follow the steps below.

List your major alternatives down the left side of the chart. Across the top of the chart fill in the categories of information you believe are important to your decision. This is usually a personal matter. We have different values, priorities, and worries, so we often give serious consideration to different types of information when considering alternatives. Someone who did not care particularly about the appearance of a car might not include that category. Someone who cared a great deal about a model's mechanical reliability would add an additional category for that set of information. No matter how many categories you wish to consider, list them separately across the top (with vertical lines added). The chart will now look like the one at the top of the next page.

Choices	Initial Cost	Looks/ Style	Gas Mileage	Disk Brakes
Cadillac				
Chevrolet				
Toyota				
Ford				

Fill in the information in the chart. You may put the information in the cells of the chart in many ways: checkmarks, numbers, symbols, scales or codes, words, or whatever else makes sense to you. A general rule is to make the information as specific as you can while still being able to show the big picture, but remember that you make these charts for your convenience. Below is an example of a completed classification chart.

Choices	Initial Cost	Looks/ Style	Gas Mileage	Disk Brakes
Cadillac	$16,950	Impressive	Yes	
Chevrolet	$10,200	Fair	27 mpg	No
Toyota	$7,500	Okay	39 mpg	Yes
Ford	$7,950	Sleek	35 mpg	Yes

In columns 1 and 4, we used exact information about cost and mileage. Why? Because precise figures were most useful, and we had the information. In column 2 we used a word scale. Why? Because this and many other types of information are not definite. We make our own judgement about a car's appearance, and choose a scale which fits that judgement. In column 5, we used only yes or no, because each car either has or does not have disk brakes.

You will use all of these methods at one time or another. For each type of information in a classification chart, choose the method that is most accurate, yet most useful for your purposes. The goal is to display very clearly each piece of information that is relevant to your alternatives. Fill in the cells in whatever way will best accomplish that goal.

Notice two things about the chart on the previous page. First, it does not include all of the information you have; information about riding comfort is missing. Draw a set of cells to the right of those in the last chart, and fill them in to indicate your ratings of the riding comfort of the various cars.

Second, notice that the cell where the "Cadillac" row meets the "miles per gallon" row is empty. The blank space suggests that you need to do more research in order to find that particular piece of missing information.

When you have filled in all the information on a classification chart, you have relieved your mind of the need to keep track of all those facts. Often, you have also identified other types of information you want and other alternatives you might consider. Frequently a first chart, to relieve the memory pressure on your brain, leads to more elaborate charts as you begin to actively think things through.

At least you will have organized your information in a manner that makes clear what you know about your choices and how they compare. Then you are ready to evaluate the information and make a decision. It is easier to make those decisions when the information is displayed on a chart than when it is juggled in your mind.

Exercise 9a

Grouping Job Applicants

Tomas is personnel officer for a large corporation which has manufacturing plants in several cities. He is stationed at corporate headquarters in St. Louis. One of his jobs is to match job applicants with available jobs.

One of the job areas with which he is concerned is a particular type of electronics assembler. He has a list of people in the St. Louis area who have applied for that kind of job. He has to match them with openings when they occur in any of the plants. Below are listed the current applicants for jobs as electronics assemblers:

George Carter — 18 years old; no experience; will work any shift; willing to move.

Sandy Duncan — 5 years experience; can work second shift only; 26 years old; must stay in St. Louis.

Bert Bender — must stay in St. Louis; 46; cannot work third shift; 27 years experience.

Daniel Lee — 19 years old; no experience; will move; will work any shift.

Marvin Prince — 32 years old; second shift only; 10 years experience; will not move.

Tecoi Matthews — 25 years experience; first shift only; 49 years old; will not work more than 30 miles away from St. Louis.

Edwin Rivers — will move; 3 years experience; 31; can work any shift.

Charles Williams	—	must work in St. Louis; 57 years old; can only work second or third shift; 5 years experience.
Victoria Adkins	—	can work first or second shift; willing to move; 47 years old; 22 years experience.
Evelyn Jacobs	—	will not move; 6 years experience; can work any shift; 29 years old.
Lauretta Banks	—	16 years experience; 48 years old; can only work second shift; cannot leave St. Louis.
Glena Evans	—	no experience; 19 years old; can work any shift; can move anywhere (but prefers small towns).
Monterio Patterson	—	can only work first or third shift; 38 years old; cannot work more than 40 miles from St. Louis.
Julia Prosperity	—	42 years old; 16 years experience; can work any shift, anywhere.
Tricia Smith	—	1 year experience; would prefer third shift; can move; 19 years old.
Gregory Paine	—	2 years experience; cannot move; 28 years old; can work any shift.

1. On Monday afternoon, one of the local plants puts in a request for an electronics assembler. They specify that the person must have at least 5 years of experience and be able to work any shift. Put these names into two categories, based on those job requirements.

Discuss what was difficult about this assignment with the class or your team.

2. On a separate sheet of paper, create a classification chart which includes all of these applicants and the key information about them. When you finish, compare charts with others in the class and discuss any differences.

3. On Tuesday, at about noon, Tomas gets another request. This is from a plant in Sikeston, Missouri (200 miles from St. Louis). They want an electronics assembler for third shift, and will train the person provided he or she has at least a year's experience. Use your classification chart to decide which persons Tomas can recommend.

Was this task simpler to complete than the first one? Was the task itself simpler, or did the classification chart make it quicker to do?

4. On Thursday afternoon Tomas gets a third request. This is for an electronics assembler with moderate (more than five years) experience who is willing to move to the Chicago area. Which applicants would Tomas suggest?

Think About It

What two or three Thinking Tools seem most important when you try to create a **classification chart**?

5. Tomas has a final request on Thursday. A new plant in Alaska needs two electronics assemblers. They would like several years of experience and would prefer that the two people be as young as possible, since conditions are very rugged there. Based on the information given, list the people Tomas should recommend. Put them in priority order.

Exercise 9b

Organizing A Schedule

Diana is in charge of scheduling for Elliott Industries, Inc. — a small company that makes specialty china. She is trying to plan the employees' work schedule for the next two months. She has 12 workers and four jobs to fill on each of three shifts. She must have a trained EMT (Emergency Medical Technician) working on each shift.

Below are listed the twelve employees, and some information about them.

Smith — can work shifts 1 and 3; can work as a Setter or a Machine Operator; does not get specialist's pay; is 32 years old.

Tanney — 47; can work shifts 2 or 3; can work as a Setter or Packer; gets specialist's pay; not an EMT.

DiDiego — can only work third shift; can work as a Machine Operator or Setter; 55 years old; gets specialist's pay.

Ho — 29 years old; gets specialist's pay; works as a Machine Operator or Marker; a trained EMT; can work shifts 1 and 3.

Offutt — can work shifts 2 and 3; trained as a Packer and Marker; 64 years old; will retire in 3 months; gets specialist's pay; not an EMT.

Ferguson — is a trained EMT, but gets no specialist's pay; can only work first shift; can work as a Packer or Marker; 47 years old.

Padilla — can work shifts 1 or 2, but not both; trained as a Machine Operator or Packer; no specialist's pay; age unknown.

Quade — can only work as a Setter; could work any shift last year, but now can only work second shift; a trained EMT; 39; no specialist's pay.

Odell — must work third shift, if at all; trained as a Packer; just certified as an EMT; 57 years old; receives specialist's pay.

Jackson — trained as a Machine Operator, though in training for Packer; can work shifts 1 or 2; no specialist's pay; trained as an EMT.

Emerson — can work as a Machine Operator or Marker; not an EMT, and no specialist's pay; can only work first shift because wife works second; not a trained EMT.

Jefferson — not a trained EMT; 58 years old; receives specialist's pay; can only work second shift right now; can work as a Marker.

1. On a separate page, make a classification chart to organize the information about these workers.

2. By yourself or with a team, figure out who Diana should assign to each shift to meet the requirements. List them below:

   Those scheduled for First shift are:

   Those scheduled for Second shift are:

   Those scheduled for Third shift are:

Share your answers with the class; discuss any differences.

3. Describe below the method you used to figure out who should be assigned to each shift. Then discuss your methods — and what was difficult about this assignment — with the class.

This exercise required you to use many Thinking Tools. **Which ones** did you use?

5. When does a person need to do this kind of organizing? Think of two or more situations in a college where it is important to organize people's time. List them below, and the factors that have to be considered.

Situation 1:

Situation 2:

Exercise 9c

Choosing Among Three Employees For A Promotion

Emory Boyd is Business Director for Action Products, Inc. His responsibilities include personnel, bookkeeping, payroll, scheduling, records, word processing, and shipping and receiving. Last week his Office Manager had a nervous breakdown and quit to retire to her farm in West Virginia. Emory now has to pick a replacement Office Manager. He has three main candidates, as follow:

George Willis

17 years with Action Products; the payroll supervisor (the largest, most critical area); cheerful and cooperative; very neat and orderly, and able to create a system for everything; tends to go to pieces when asked to handle situations in which his systems do not work; bookish, and tends to like to work by himself among his books and ledgers; probably the most intelligent of Emory's staff members; always friendly and responsive when someone involves him in office activities, but never volunteers to lead; respected and well liked by the staff.

Glenda James

13 years with the company; production scheduler; works well under pressure with something new always going on; a bit cross and demanding, especially when someone questions her orders in times of crisis; knows almost everything about the many business office activities; ambitious; willing to work long hours; a leader in terms of suggesting new methods; impatient with policies and rules when a problem looms; likes to do everything herself instead of delegating responsibility; out to prove herself; generally respected, but resented and disliked by some staff.

Terry Peters

5 years with the company; a college graduate (in Business Administration); began as an employee relations clerk and is now personnel assistant; helpful to everyone; well-liked and seen as a "comer"; takes responsibility and carries it out well; a very quick learner; has some chronic health problems; someone whom people go to for ideas, advice and help; hard working; perhaps tries a bit too hard to be friendly and liked.

Which one of these would be Emory's best bet as an Office Manager? You may have an opinion, but before giving it set up a classification chart on a separate sheet to organize your information about these three people.

1. Having organized your information, which person would you personally recommend that Emory choose for the job? Why?

2. Which person would you pick if you wanted someone:

   - who could solve sudden problems quickly and accurately? Why?

   - who would keep the operation running smoothly and normally? Why?

   - who could motivate others to do their very best? Why?

3. Did you think that Terry was a man or a woman?

   Why? And would it matter in your decision? Discuss this with others.

Exercise 9d

Organizing Charts For Some Practical Situations

Classification charts help us pick jobs, organize reports, solve math problems and make many of the other decisions which affect our lives. We too often think of writing information down only when it is too late. It seems very academic and artificial, somehow, to abandon our mental juggling act and write down relevant information in a systematic way. However, taking that step is often the difference between a good and a poor choice. That can matter a great deal with important decisions.

1. Many students pursue an education in order to eventually develop a satisfying career. Students attending two-year colleges often choose programs that lead directly to a career. Students going to a four-year college or university often study more general subjects which lead indirectly to a career.

   Below is information about two graduates. Pick either student and on a separate sheet organize his or her choices in terms of the things to consider about that job. You do not have to fill in the cells.

   a. Rennie is graduating from Sandstone Junior College in computer programming. Her placement office suggests that she apply for four different jobs: computer data entry operator, computer operator, programming assistant and microcomputer technician. Organize a chart for her, comparing aspects of the jobs which she should consider.

   b. Mannie is graduating from Parthenon State College in political science. His placement office suggests that he apply for four different jobs: speech writer, political assistant, aide, and writer. Organize a chart for him, comparing the aspects he should consider.

As a team or class, decide how organizing a chart like this might help Mannie or Rennie make a job choice.

2. Every college student has to write papers. Classification charts can sometimes be a help in this task, too. For example, let's say you are going to write a paper on the topic *Ways to lead a group*. You might think of three alternative ways of leading groups: give orders (dictator), talk until everyone agrees (consensus), or take votes (democratic). Those might be the alternatives to list down the side of the chart. Then you might think about factors in group leadership that these alternatives would affect: efficiency of decisions, group support, prestige, use of time, and so on. Those might be the information categories to list across the top of the chart. Fill in such a chart below.

3. Kevin must write a four-page paper for his English class. He is given three choices of topics, and in the paper he must compare the various aspects of the topic. His choices are:

   a. ways of generating electrical power;
   b. ways of decreasing pollution; or
   c. ways of conserving energy.

   To help Kevin, pick one of his three choices, and prepare a classification chart on a separate sheet. List the alternatives down the side and the factors you will consider across the top. You do not have to fill in the cells.

   a How would Kevin's classification chart help you do the research for this paper?

   b. How would this classification chart help you write the paper, once you had done the research?

4. Here is another situation. A man must decide whether or not to retire; it is not an easy choice. Make a classification chart that helps to organize the choice.

Mike Monroney is a computer specialist with the U.S. Marine Corps. He has nearly completed his 20-year enlistment. That means that he can retire from the Marine Corps and draw a good percentage of his current pay for the rest of his life. However, the Marines will help his children through college if he reenlists. All of his (and most of his wife's and children's) friends are associated with the Marines. Mike likes his job in the Marine Corps.

For a long time Mike has also wanted to be on his own. He likes electronics and computers and knows how profitable a business this can be. He has taken several business courses and would love to run his own shop, specializing in computer repair.

Mike is good with his hands and his mind, but not so good working with people. His wife, however, loves working with people — and is good at it. She would like to move back near her parents, uncles and larger family. But she also wants to put her children through college. The children are nearly old enough for college. That will cost a lot while it decreases the number of family members who might help with a new business.

a. On a separate page, organize a classification chart that would help Mike deal with his problem.

b. What would you do in this situation?

c. Why would you do that in this situation?

d. Share your answers with others in your class and discuss them.

Think About Mike's Choice

What Thinking Tools will Mike
be using as he tries to decide?

Homework

Find at least two situations in which you must make a choice and in which using a classification chart might help you. On a separate sheet of paper, describe the situations and draw one of the appropriate classification charts.

Exercise 9e

Organizing A Highly Emotional Situation

Emotion-laden situations are usually the most difficult to deal with in terms of information because our values, guilts, needs, wants, fears and hopes keep getting in the way as we try to make a decision. Often it seems cruel and heartless even to talk about information and facts in an emotional situation. People might judge us (or we might judge ourselves) to be uncaring, unloving and cold.

Yet, systematically organizing information in charts or other ways can actually be a help in such situations. Organization can get the facts down in black and white. It can help identify more facts that we do not have but need. Organizing information can remove some of our confusion and help us admit what is often the most important choice of all: "the facts say this, but my heart says that!" Then we can at least be honest about what the real choice might be.

Below is an emotional situation. It is one that many people have faced or will face in one form or another.

> Your Uncle John lives with you. He is 58 years old. He has been your father figure for a number of years. This morning, he had a very severe reaction to a medication he recently started taking. He went into convulsions, lapsed into a coma, and has not recovered consciousness since then (ten hours ago).
>
> Your family doctor was at the hospital when the ambulance brought John to the emergency room. It is a small hospital in a rural area. Your uncle's pulse, brain waves, and other vital signs have varied widely since he was admitted. Your doctor has told you that he thinks your uncle has a rare, and very dangerous, medical reaction. He estimates that your uncle will probably die if he is not put on very specialized medical equipment within the next 18 hours.

Unfortunately, the nearest place that has this equipment is 190 miles away at a hospital in Perry City. Your doctor says that if his diagnosis is correct, your uncle will have to be kept on that equipment permanently. He says he remembers an article in a medical journal which suggested that the recovery rate from this problem is very poor, but that some people have recovered their speech, some movement and part of their mental abilities. He does not know what the equipment costs, but you suspect that it is very expensive.

You are a college student, attending on a financial-need grant. You are married and the parent of a 2-year-old child and your spouse works. Your family lives nearby. Traditionally, they have been of very little help in an emergency but nonetheless very free with their opinions and judgements after the crisis is over.

This is a difficult situation, but a common one. It mixes hard facts and deep emotions. Below, organize the situation into an information chart. As you do, remember that guilt, others' opinions, and similar considerations are also information categories. Also, realize that you have more than two alternatives.

Good luck.

1. List any other information that you would like to have before you make a choice and where you might get it.

2. Given this information, what choice do you think you would make in this situation?

   I would ...

3. Why would you make that choice?

4. Share your answers with others in the class and discuss them. List below any good answers or ideas which other students suggest.

5. Did making a classification chart help you sort out the facts and feelings a little bit? Why or how?

6. If you wish, poll the class to see if anyone has faced a situation similar to this one. If so, that student might describe how decisions were made (or not made) in that situation and whether or not a more systematic way of organizing the factors on paper would have helped.

Exercise 9f

Classification Charts On The Job

Dee works in an electronics assembly plant as a technician. She has worked there for seven years and has tried very hard to move up. During that time she completed a degree in electronic engineering technology at night at a local technical college, despite having a husband and child. She is determined to be a success in the company and hopes to be promoted to supervisor during the next year.

Today Dee is leaving work with two co-workers, one a new employee and the other the son of a local politician. As they near the door, the shift supervisor stops them. He says that there has been frequent theft of equipment parts recently, and today there will be an inspection of everyone's toolkit before they leave. The politician's son, a bully and loudmouth, but influential in the plant, immediately says, "No way are you going to inspect my toolkit. I'm leaving now! And I'm sure my friends here agree with me!"

Dee has only a few seconds to figure out what to do — agree to the search, agree with the co-worker, or think of something else. Sometimes people can do a lot of thinking in a few seconds. Think of several things Dee could say or do in this situation. Think of the implications of those actions (such as effect on job and supervisor's opinion).

How do you make a classification chart from this situation? List Dee's alternative courses of action down the left side of the paper. Then list the implications and factors across the top. Fill in the cells by considering how each alternative affects, or is affected by, those implications and factors. Make the chart on a separate page.

1. What should Dee do? Explain why your chart suggests that this is the best solution.

2. Share your chart and answers with others in the class.

Exercise 9g

Using Thinking Tools With Complex Information

Information usually looks so simple after it is organized. And it often looks so hopeless and confusing before it is organized. Bringing order out of confusing information is one of the most important and complicated of human activities. Thinking Tools play an important part in that activity.

1. Imagine any room in your house that often gets messy. If you work you might want to imagine your work area or your desk. Either way, focus your mind on a physical space that is very messy.

   Now imagine yourself cleaning up that area. Imagine what you will do to make it neat. Imagine the decisions you will make. List some of those decisions and actions below.

   Think about the Thinking Tools you used to make that imaginary space neat. How did you decide where to start? How did you figure out what went where? How did you tackle the job? How did you decide when you were finished? Below, list the Thinking Tools you used in that imaginary situation.

2. With other students, review the exercises in this chapter and list the Thinking Tools you found yourself using. For each one describe how you used that tool. The *how* is very important. It is easy to say that a carpenter used a hammer. It is much harder — and much more important — to explain how he used it to create a beautiful cabinet. How did you use your Thinking Tools to create a beautiful solution?

   - One Thinking Tool that I used was:

     And here is how I used it:

   - A second Thinking Tool that I used was:

     And here is how I used it:

   - A third Thinking Tool that I used was:

     And here is how I used it:

   - A fourth Thinking Tool that I used was:

     And here is how I used it:

3. Finally, look at the Thinking Tools you listed in parts 1 and 2 on the previous page. Compare them. Were the Tools mainly the same? Discuss the similarities and differences between tools for cleaning up a messy room and tools for organizing information into charts.

   a. Which ones were mostly the same? Why?

   b. Which ones were mostly different? Why?

   c. Pick out your best Thinking Tools for organizing information usefully in charts and put them in the box below.

Think About It!

What are your best thinking tools for solving these problems?

Supplemental Exercise 9h

Structuring Information Through Note-Taking

1. Students spend most of their class time taking notes. Teachers lecture or demonstrate, and students write it down. Some students write down everything a teacher says; some write down only a few things. Either way, most students take some sort of notes in the classroom. There is surely some reason for all of this effort going into note-taking. Answer the question below, as a team; list as many different answers as you can.

   Why is taking notes useful in a course?

2. Hopefully you identified four or five reasons because there are at least that many. You may have listed a reason something like this one: *to pass the test.* That is a very worthwhile, honest reason for taking notes, but it leads to another set of questions: What do you do with the notes? How do they help you pass the tests? How can you restructure the notes so they are most useful to you?

   Taking notes is one step toward passing a test. But it is not the last step. The next step is to synthesize (pull together) all the information you have. You need to reorganize the notes and eliminate minor information. Imagine taking 30 pages of notes during eight class periods and compressing them into three note cards. You could study those three cards and be fully ready for the test.

The question is: what would those three note cards contain? The question below is another way of asking this. It is the second step in structuring information through note taking. Two possible answers are given; see if you can list five more.

What are the characteristics of a good set of compressed notes? They

a. include everything the teacher has highlighted.

b. anticipate the kinds of questions the teacher asks.

c.

d.

e.

f.

g.

3. Can you magically create a set of compressed notes that meet the standards you listed above? Of course not. Developing compressed notes is like going to a distant city — to be sure you get there, you must plan ahead. You need to know where you are going and then figure out how to get there. In this case, you first need to know what kind of information, in what form, you will need. Then you can be sure to get it and organize it correctly.

Therefore, the third important question is raised in three parts as follows. Examples of some answers are given. With your team, add three more items to each part.

a. What can I do to structure the information after class once I have taken the notes?

- Compare the class notes with the textbook information.
-
-
-

b. What can I do during class to be sure that I have all the information?

- Listen for overall concepts or ideas, and note the specific examples or evidences of them.
-
-
-

c. What can I do before class to make sure that I can take proper notes?

- Think of questions relating to the text readings so I can figure out what the teacher might talk about.
-
-
-

4. Above, you listed many things you could do to structure your note taking. Now take all of those items from step 3 and decide how often you, personally, practice them.

Note-taking actions I usually take are:

Note-taking actions I occasionally take are:

Note-taking actions I do not take are:

5. To take good notes, you must listen, think and write all at the same time. How do Thinking Tools help with that?

Chapter Ten

Thinking With Sequences

We draw on background knowledge. We rely on what seems right. We find clue words. We use logic or context. There are many ways of thinking which help us know how to sequence something.

A sequence is the order of things — first, second, third. Many things happen in sequences: first you do this; then you do that; then you do the last thing. We start cars with a certain sequence of actions, and we cook using sequences of tasks. We organize courses or papers in sequences, and we solve problems in sequences. Recognizing a good sequence and being able to put things into a good sequence are very important skills in school and life.

This chapter will help you improve several sequence skills. After completing it, you will be better able to:

- ❑ recognize sequence clues;
- ❑ arrange sentences, words, numbers in sequences;
- ❑ solve problems in sequences
- ❑ recognize Thinking Tools to use with sequences.

All of us already know how to judge many things in terms of sequences. Would you know that something was wrong if a friend started to fry an egg before breaking the shell? Tried to remove a flat tire before using the jack? What if your teacher tried to give the final exam on the first day of class? You would know that something was wrong because the sequence would be wrong.

Recognizing, making and using sequences happens in many ways. We draw on our background knowledge. We depend on what seems right.

We find clue words in written or spoken sentences and we use logic. There are many techniques which help us manipulate sequences.

Using sequences naturally becomes a more difficult task as we deal with more complex forms of knowledge. For example, very complex equipment can be operated only in a certain sequence of steps — think of a missile countdown. Understanding a theory of human action depends on being able to follow several steps in a chain of thought. Making a good judgement about a technical report depends on following a sequence of clues through many paragraphs.

In college, your natural ability to use sequences at the level of eggs, tires and tests will be challenged very strongly. You will need to strengthen your ability to recognize and use sequences in ways that will pay off in your classes and elsewhere.

As we begin this chapter, think about a Thinking Tool which is very important with sequences — key words. Spend a few moments imagining yourself giving someone instructions.

Choose one of these situations: changing a tire, cooking an egg, riding a bicycle or driving a car. Right now, think through the directions you would give the other person.

After you have had that mental conversation, try to think of the key words you used to show parts of the sequence. With others in the class, list as many key sequence words as you can, based on imagining yourself giving those directions. Two examples are given.

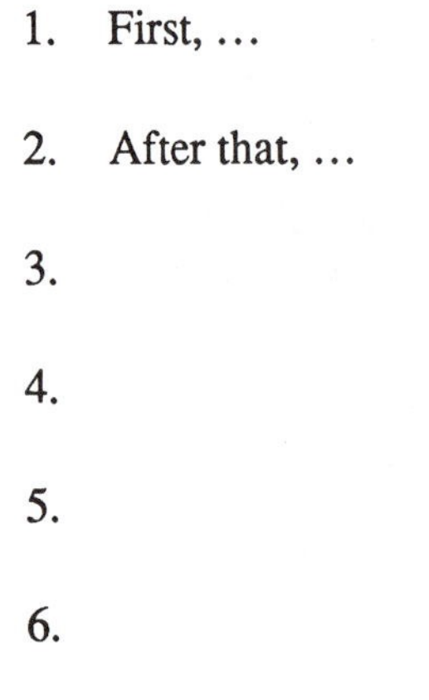

1. First, ...
2. After that, ...
3.
4.
5.
6.

Exercise 10a

Textbook Clues To Sequence

Writers of textbooks, cookbooks, operator's manuals, and many other types of books use sequences to explain their processes, procedures and events. They explain and describe things in terms of sequences of activities. The sentences below were taken from college textbooks. Locate the words in the sentences (if any) that signal the beginning of a sequence. Underline those words.

1. The events leading to the historic battle of Bunker Hill were ...
2. All financial revolutions have economic causes, such as ...
3. Geologic development may be observed by studying these different periods in our history ...
4. Previewing a textbook chapter is a very brief process that begins with a look at the chapter title and then, ...
5. Job security depends on such situations as ...
6. A very strange set of coincidences led to the beginning of the Third Crusade. They were ...
7. The five steps in getting a job are ...
8. Reading problems in math requires a procedure similar to reading any text assignment:
9. There are several different, conflicting theories to explain the sudden fight in the dormitory:
10. You can break the math anxiety chain by following these basic steps:
11. Since we will be referring constantly to this concept let us walk through it carefully:
12. The following phases will guide you in the right direction in preparing research papers:

13. Seven theories have been suggested to explain the rise of the Roman Empire, as follow:

14. It is important that the following procedure be followed in preparing a trial balance:

15. In the months between Lincoln's election in November, 1860 and the outbreak of war in April, 1861, the fate of the Union was decided by a series of events:

16. To write the chemical equation that represents a chemical reaction you must proceed in steps that satisfy the three factors in equation writing:

17. A chemical reaction may occur in a sequence called the reaction pathway or reaction mechanism, as follows:

18. Four famous American presidents played important roles in the opening of the West. They were ...

First, share your answers with others in the class and discuss them.

Second, answer this question: Why is it helpful to be able to identify key words to sequences in a textbook?

Homework

Take any textbook from one of your classes. Look through it and find at least four sentences that give you sequence clues like the ones above. Write them below.

- ❑
- ❑
- ❑
- ❑

Exercise 10b

A Sequence For Production

When industries make a product, they use a sequence of events. Manufacturers employ specialists to find the best possible sequence — the one that is quickest, cheapest and most reliable. Below is an industrial sequence for making Squawls. For each step, underline the key words or phrases which tell where that step fits into the total process.

To make Squawls,

1. Pellets of metal are first sorted by size.
2. The different sizes are then divided and shipped to separate parts of the plant to make different types of Squawls.
3. After dividing, they are welded to stainless steel bars.
4. The stainless steel bars are then coated with a special magnetic material.
5. The magnetically coated bars are then polished with reflecting shellac.
6. Next, the polished bars are exposed to temperatures below zero degrees for at least 11 hours.
7. Following the freezing operation they are dropped into a boiling acid bath.
8. After the acid bath they are dried for 48 hours.
9. The fully dried bars are then exposed to blowing sand particles.
10. Next, the sanded bars are shaken in a vibrator.
11. Before the plastic coating, they are radiated for 32 minutes.
12. Once they are radiated, the bars are dipped into a plastic coating.

13. When finished, the Squawls are stamped with the company's trademark.

14. The Squawls are then wrapped in individual foil packets.

15. Afterwards, the stamped Squawls are packed 43 to a carton.

16. Finally they are shipped to distributors.

After you have underlined the key phrases or words, think about what you have done. As a class, discuss these questions:

1. How do you know that those are the right clues?

2. What alerts you to the "key" phrases or words?

Write your answers in the space below.

No one is certain of exactly how we become alert to mental cues, but a few things do seem clear. Partly this ability depends on a person's breadth of experience. Partly it depends on a person's skills in manipulating Thinking Tools. Partly it depends on awareness of the kinds of clues that are available in written material.

You perhaps noticed that there were at least two types of clues in those sentences: **direct clues** — the words "first", "finally", etc., and **context clues** — the clues that depend on what went before and after that particular sentence. These clues often repeat information found in the previous sentence.

Which of the 16 sentences have direct clues, and which of them have context clues? Write your answers below.

1. The sentences containing direct clues were numbered:

2. The sentences containing context clues were numbered:

Exercise 10c

Unscrambling Short Sequences

Often we can think of many actions which must be taken in a given situation. The difficult part sometimes is figuring out the order in which to do them: the most efficient and effective sequence. The following groups of sentences belong to a sequence, but their order is scrambled. Your task is to sort them out and show the proper sequence by numbering them correctly. How do you do that? Use a combination of clue words, common sense and experience.

1. Here is a sequence for creating a topic sentence for a paper. Put the numbers 1 through 4 in front of the four statements to show the proper order.

    ____ a. Next, select one of the topics and limit it so that it can be developed into a short paper.

    ____ b. Narrow your subject to several possible writing topics that deal with the general subject.

    ____ c. To develop a thesis statement, first decide upon your general subject and narrower topic.

    ____ d. Transform the limited topic chosen into several versions of thesis sentences that may be effective.

Share your answers with your team and explain why you chose that particular sequence. What clues did you use?

2. In this situation the topic of the scrambled sentences is changing the oil filter on your car. Mark the sentences 1 through 5 to indicate the proper sequence.

   ____ a. Apply a thin film of oil to the new filter gasket.

   ____ b. Tighten the new filter with a filter wrench.

   ____ c. Install the filter on the engine mount.

   ____ d. Then remove the old oil filter and gasket from the engine mount.

   ____ e. To change the oil filter, first drain the old engine oil out of the engine.

3. The topic of this scrambled sequence is underlining a book. List the tasks as numbers 1 through 6.

   ____ a. Recite the ideas you wish to underline in your own words before underlining anything.

   ____ b. Have a cumulative review of what you read and underlined each week in each course after you have finished all underlining.

   ____ c. Underline enough words and phrases from the selection to form your own sentences.

   ____ d. Read the whole text selection before even starting to plan your underlining strategy.

   ____ e. Recite and review the material you edited and underlined at the end of each text-reading session.

   ____ f. After underlining a section, edit it by using the margin to explain, organize, outline, summarize or question.

Discuss this question with others in the class: what aspects of deciphering the above sequences were most difficult and why? Write your answers below.

4. Planning your time is an important academic skill. Good students tend to organize their time carefully in order to get the important things done well before doing less important things. Number these time-management steps as 1 through 5 in sequence.

____ a. Next to each item on your list put down the estimated time it will take you to do it.

____ b. Begin making a time schedule by filling in all the fixed hours in your day.

____ c. Before you designate specific times for accomplishing homework look at the fixed hours and note when you have free time.

____ d. The next step is to make a list of all the things you must do during the next week.

____ e. Then look at your "to do" list and fit in all the other tasks in the time available.

5. This scrambled exercise is about vocabulary cards — a technique for quickly learning new words in any technical area. Indicate the sequence of steps with numbers 1 through 6.

____ a. Prepare and study the cards daily and weekly.

____ b. Write new vocabulary words on 3 x 5 cards, and write the definitions on the back.

____ c. Overlearn the cards by going through them two or three times after you are able to do them perfectly.

____ d. Restudy the ones you did not know.

____ e. Self-test yourself frequently in short study sessions.

____ f. Sort the cards into two stacks: the ones you know and the ones you have not completely learned.

Explain below how common sense and logic helped you reorganize the sequence of that set of sentences. How did you figure out which sentence went first, second, third?

Think About Sequences

List several Thinking Tools that you use when **unscrambling sequences of steps.**

Exercise 10d

Unscrambling Directions

Directions are a major form of sequences. Usually, when you are given directions they are in a particular order. In this exercise you must figure out directions on a map. It might make you feel more secure to have an atlas or a map of the United States to refer to while working this first activity. However, you do not need it; there are enough clues built into the sentences to let you determine the sequence.

1. In this situation you are given scrambled directions for traveling from Kansas City, Kansas, to Tacoma, Washington. Your job is to unscramble the instructions. Put a "1" before the first part of the sequence, a "2" before the second part, and so on until you have all the directions in order.

____ a. After Rock Springs, Wyoming, go west to Salt Lake City.

____ b. Now take I90 across Montana to Coeur d'Alene.

____ c. Drive from Kansas City to Hays.

____ d. Then go west across most of Wyoming to Rock Springs.

____ e. Go west and then south to Tacoma, Washington.

____ f. Seventh, go north from Idaho into Montana to Butte.

____ g. Third, go north from Denver to Cheyenne, Wyoming.

____ h. From Coeur d'Alene, move west into Spokane, Washington.

____ i. Then go west to Denver, Colorado.

____ j. Next, go north into Idaho to Pocatello.

Think about how you deciphered the sequence. What kind of clues did you find in each sentence: direct or context clues? Put D before any sentence that had a direct clue and C before each one that had a context clue (some sentences may have both).

2. This exercise will prove that you do not need detailed knowledge of geography, maps or place names to unscramble some map sequences. The names of real cities and states have been replaced with the names of woods and metals. Nevertheless, you will be able to unscramble the sequence simply by using key words and context clues. Write down the order of the directions from 1 to 10.

____ a. Ninth, we will leave Ambergris and arrive at Iron, Fir.

____ b. Next, we will take I20 from Bronze to Gold, Silver.

____ c. Then we will go east on US 72 to Tin, Aluminum.

____ d. Second, we will drive from Steel to Oak, Plywood.

____ e. Finally, we will go west from Iron and arrive at Pine, Cedar.

____ f. The problem here is that we need to drive from Steel to Pine, Cedar.

____ g. Fifth, after Tin, we will go on US 29 and I85 to Bronze, Aluminum.

____ h. Next, let's go from Maple to Mahogany, Ambergris.

____ i. Then we will go from Oak to Cherry, Aluminum.

____ j. Seventh, we will drive to Maple on the western edge of Silver.

Once again, put D (direct clue) and/or C (context clue) in front of each sentence to identify the kind of clue which helped you resequence those directions. Share your answers with others in the class. Also discuss what this activity emphasized about the power of context clues in sequencing.

Homework

You will need to have a map of the western U.S. Figure out how to drive from Los Angeles, California to Detroit, Michigan (from the greatest user of cars to the greatest builder of cars). Write down ten steps in the journey using clue words. Then rewrite those ten steps in scrambled order. Trade with someone and put each other's scrambled sequence back in order.

Exercise 10e

Unscrambling Academic Sequences

Many assignments and situations in college are based on sequences. Unfortunately, very often we do not recognize the sequence, so we cannot use it to our advantage. This exercise may help sensitize you to the academic sequences occurring around you.

1. Kendall has decided to look into some area colleges after being thrown out on his ear from his parents' house for lying around all day doing nothing. His parents will let him back in the house only if he enrolls in college or gets a job. Kendall refuses to get a job. Crazy Rick, Kendall's friend, tries to explain the registration procedure to him, but as usual Rick's information is all mixed up. Below are listed the 14 things that Rick says (the ones that make any sense at all). Your job is to sequence them for Kendall by putting "1" before the first step in the sequence, "2" before the second step, and so forth.

____ a. You have to find out when registration is held.

____ b. You investigate several colleges' programs and costs.

____ c. You find out when and where your first class is held.

____ d. You start learning from your instructor.

____ e. You decide to apply to Rigorous TEC.

____ f. You pay all your fees for the fall quarter.

____ g. You apply at Rigorous TEC.

____ h. You find the classroom for your first class.

____ i. You register for your fall quarter courses.

____ j. You have to decide whether you want to go to college or starve.

____ k. You arrange to get to school on time the first day.

____ l. You take the placement test after applying and being accepted.

____ m. You pick a seat in your classroom.

____ n. Once accepted, you decide to start classes in the fall quarter.

Compare your answers with those of others in your class. Defend any different answers you have, remembering that opinions often vary about the proper sequence.

As a team, list from your own experience several other steps which actually occur in the registration process. Show where each new step occurs in the sequence by writing such things as "after c", "before m", and so forth.

With the class, discuss how you organized your work on this problem. Discuss what techniques were easiest. Summarize your favorite approach here, writing out your system in enough detail that someone else could read it and follow it.

2. Writing a research paper for a business course requires that you use a writing process you might use in writing any type of research paper. The sequence below has those steps in scrambled order. Sort out the 15 steps in the process and indicate which is first, second, third, and so forth by writing the numbers in the spaces before each step. Use both direct clues and context clues in deciding the order.

____ a. Decide on my major content for the paper.

____ b. Get the information I need to fit into the outline.

____ c. Finish my first draft of the paper.

____ d. Get my assignment: to write a research paper.

____ e. Lay out the general structure or outline of the paper.

____ f. Revise my draft paper for grammar.

____ g. Revise my draft paper for content.

____ h. Have my instructor approve my topic.

____ i. Do some initial reading on the content areas I have chosen.

____ j. Turn in my final paper.

____ k. Write my first draft of most of the paper.

____ l. Rewrite my first draft, several times if necessary.

____ m. Pick a topic for my assigned paper.

____ n. Take some initial notes on the content areas I have chosen.

____ o. Get additional information to fill in the gaps in my first draft.

Was this a particularly difficult sequence to unscramble? If so, decide why it was harder than some others and write out what the difficulties were.

See if grouping will help. By looking at the sequence on the previous page, you can figure out that it has about three stages. List the letters of the sentences on the previous page under the proper stage.

Start	Organize/Research	Write

How could you use these stages to make it easier to find the sequence, tackling each stage separately?

Share your answers with others in the class. Explain your reasons for answering as you did and listen carefully to others' explanations. Change your answers if you wish, but defend your thoughts if you think you have good reasons for what you wrote.

Think About It!

What Thinking Tools did you use, and how did you use them while **unscrambling these sequences**?

Exercise 10f

Sequences In Finding A Job

Here is another scrambled sequence. We are dealing with the steps you take in order to find a good job. Arrange these steps in sequence from 1 to 20 by writing the numbers in the space before each step.

____ a. Look for jobs in the help-wanted ads, your college's placement office and/or an employment agency.

____ b. Before you begin your job search, you should analyze your marketable skills, your experience and your personal preferences in order to identify your job objectives.

____ c. After arriving at the interview, use good manners and formal English; address the interviewers as "Mr.", "Mrs.", "Ms." or "Miss", and use their last names.

____ d. Get to the interview on time by planning in advance for transportation, heavy traffic, locating the office and finding a place to park.

____ e. You will then perhaps get the job you want!

____ f. If nothing definite has been said before you leave the interview, ask if you should call back or wait for the company to call you.

____ g. Secondly, organize this job information in the form of a resume.

____ h. If you are invited for an interview, do some research and planning before the interview.

____ i. The next thing you should do before the interview is anticipate some questions you might be asked and plan your answers.

____ j. Answer questions in detail during the interview and ask the employer any questions you have.

____ k. After anticipating the questions you might be asked, gather the documents you will need, such as a Social Security card, your school transcript, your military records and your resume.

____ l. When you contact a reference for your resume and he or she seems reluctant to help you, do not use that person as a reference. That person might not give you a very good recommendation.

____ m. As a follow-up after the interview, write a simple business letter thanking the employer for the interview.

____ n. If a letter of application is requested to apply for a job, follow the format of a simple typed business letter, identifying the job you are applying for, your educational background, your experience, your willingness to come for an interview, and how and when you can be contacted.

____ o. If you list references on your resume, contact them for permission before you do it.

____ p. Thank the interviewer for her or his time and leave.

____ q. When you go for the interview, wear clean, neat clothes which are appropriate for the occasion.

____ r. When the interview is ending, the employer will usually thank you for coming and will stand up.

____ s. As soon as you are invited for an interview, inform yourself about the company and formulate some key questions you can ask about the business or the position.

____ t. When applying for a job from a want ad, apply in the manner indicated (resume, letter, or phone call).

When you finish the above sequence share your work with others in the class. When there is disagreement, try to resolve it by looking at the direct or context clues in the sentence under discussion.

Exercise 10g

Using Thinking Tools With Sequences

Thinking Tools are an important part of sequences, because working with sequences is a complicated mental activity. In most cases, you must use several different Thinking Tools in a certain order to work through a sequence problem. In this exercise, we will inspect the Thinking Tools we use in two different types of sequence situations. As usual, please be alert and work hard on this exercise; the amount you learn will be directly related to your effort.

1. First, let's look at sequences of directions. Remember the exercises about maps? Try to remember times when you have deciphered a set of directions putting bikes together, cooking a difficult food, finding someone's house, fixing a car. All of these involve sequences of directions.

Imagine those situations and then answer this question.

Think About Direction Sequences

List six specific Thinking Tools which you use when **giving and following directions.**

2. You have also worked a second type of sequence problem — scrambled sentences — in which you had to figure out the proper order of the steps. For these you perhaps had to use a different set of Thinking Tools.

Think About Scrambled Sequences

List several Thinking Tools which are important in **scrambled sequences** but which you did not list in the previous box.

3. As a team share and compare your answers to the previous two questions. Identify which tools were particularly important in one kind of sequence but not the other. List them below and try to explain why those Thinking Tools were particularly useful with that type of situation.

Supplemental Exercise 10h

Sequences Of Steps In Test Taking

Below are 15 scrambled steps about performing well on a test. Read through the steps thoughtfully and then follow the directions given after them.

____ a. Also, make sure you know when and where the exam is to be given.

____ b. When you receive the test read the directions twice and look over all the questions before you begin.

____ c. The best way to prepare for a test is to study well all during the term.

____ d. Having gone through the test once, go through again and do the items you checked as unsure.

____ e. Mark the questions of which you are unsure and want to go back to later.

____ f. When you go to take the test, carry the materials you will need (calculator, graph paper, pens, typing paper, etc.).

____ g. In addition, attend all class lectures, labs and discussion sessions both during the course and just before the test.

____ h. Eat sensibly before taking the test.

____ i. Proofread your paper before turning it in.

____ j. Avoid discussing the test with friends while you are waiting to take it — that will just make you more nervous.

____ k. Arrive at the test location early enough to get settled.

____ l. Sleep well the night before the test.

____ m. Make sure you know exactly what the test will cover; check with your instructor if you are in doubt.

____ n. Answer questions you are completely sure of first.

____ o. Then decide how to budget your time for each part of the test.

1. Underline the key words in each sentence. Find the words that help you identify where the item goes.

2. Which sentences contain direct clues? List them here.

3. Which sentences contain context clues? List them here.

4. As a team, identify the sequence of the 15 items. Put them in the proper order by writing the numbers 1 through 15 in front of them. If you disagree in your team, discuss your clues and your interpretations of them until you do reach agreement.

5. Finally, present your sequence to the class and listen to their sequences. If you differ, discuss the reasons for your differences.

Supplemental Exercise 10i

Unscrambling Sequences In Stories

Good writing has built-in sequences. This is true not only for famous authors; it is also true of students whose papers are returned with a grade of A. A sequence in a paper, like a road map, helps us as readers know where we were, where we are and where we are going.

How does good writing make the sequences clear? Through the types of direct and context clues you have already studied as well as through shared background knowledge. In this exercise we have "pulled apart" three short pieces of writing. Your task is to use sequencing techniques to put them back together.

1. This story about football contains ten sentences. Write the numbers 1 through 10 in front of the sentences to show the proper order.

____ a. Lombardi stared at him, the first of his breed of agents to confront the coach.

____ b. No longer is that kind of reaction possible.

____ c. An often-quoted story involves the time in 1964 when Vince Lombardi was the absolute boss of football's Green Bay Packers.

____ d. "You're in the wrong place," Lombardi told the man.

____ e. A man arrived at club headquarters and identified himself as an agent representing center Jim Ringo.

____ f. "Agent?" he questioned.

____ g. Today, for better or worse, agents are firmly ensconced at the bargaining tables of pro football.

____ h. "Mr. Ringo has just been traded to Philadelphia."

____ i. He said he wanted to negotiate a new contract for his client.

____ j. Assured of the man's identity, Lombardi retired to his office, made one phone call, and then emerged.

Compare your answers with those of others in the class, and discuss any differences. Below, summarize any major disagreements and explain the nature of the problem (differences in facts, interpretation, values, knowledge, or something else).

Would this have been easier to do if you were more familiar with football? If so, why?

2. This scrambled story is about opera, which combines music and drama — something very different from football. Again, figure out the sequence and mark the sentences 1 through 10.

____ a. "Relax, Bob," said Richard Tucker, who had made his own Met debut only 11 months ago.

____ b. Next thing I knew we were on stage, singing our way through La Traviata.

____ c. His confidence and his words made me feel better.

____ d. Suddenly, as I stood there shaking, a hand gripped my shoulder.

____ e. I felt great after it was all over!

____ f. I was scared that December in 1945 as I waited backstage to make my debut at the Metropolitan Opera in Lincoln Center, New York City.

____ g. I turned around to see a short, stocky figure with intense brown eyes and a radiant grin.

____ h. Afterwards, I knew that Richard Tucker had been right.

____ i. "There's nothing to worry about," he told me.

____ j. "You're a good singer, and you'll feel great when it's over. So let's go out there and get to it!"

Share with others and discuss any differences in your sequences. Then answer these questions.

1. Are there places in this story where the sequence of two sentences does not matter because they can be in either order? List them below.

2. If so, what does that say to you about sequences? Write your answer below.

Discuss your answers to these two questions with others in your class.

3. This final story is about a special boy. Figure out a sequence and indicate it with the numbers 1 through 8.

   ____ a. "What an irresistible smile," I thought to myself as I looked at his picture.

   ____ b. Four-fingered hands grew directly from his shoulders; his feet were attached directly to his hips.

   ____ c. A cancer surgeon, Dr. Little, had taken the picture of Juan in a hospital in Bolivia.

____ d. My first glimpse of Juan was in a photograph.

____ e. Juan was living at that hospital, not as a patient but sort of as an adopted child of the entire hospital staff.

____ f. The spirit of the boy sparkled in his eyes even at the age of eight.

____ g. The face was so vital that I didn't notice at first that Juan had no arms or legs.

____ h. The condition Juan has is known as phocomelia, a kind of deformity that very few doctors had seen in those days.

Once again, share your answers with others in the class. This one should lead to a good discussion.

Why was this passage harder than the other two? Write your answer here.

Think about the clues you found to help sort some of this passage out. How did you know how to put the following pairs of sentences in relationship to each other? Write your answers.

1. Sentence b and sentence g?

2. Sentence c and sentence d?

3. Sentence a and sentence h?

Supplemental Exercise 10j

Solving Sequences With Figure Puzzles

Here is a different kind of sequence. Below is a typical figure puzzle — the kind found often on various types of standard tests. To solve this type of puzzle requires many mental steps, or sequences of thought.

Below the puzzle are listed the 21 steps which one person used to solve this problem. There are enough clues in the words, and in the puzzle itself, for you to identify the proper sequence of steps. Use a separate page as a worksheet. When you are finished, show the proper sequence by writing the numbers 1 through 21 in front of the statements. You probably should solve this problem as a team.

Problem Which two figures are alike?

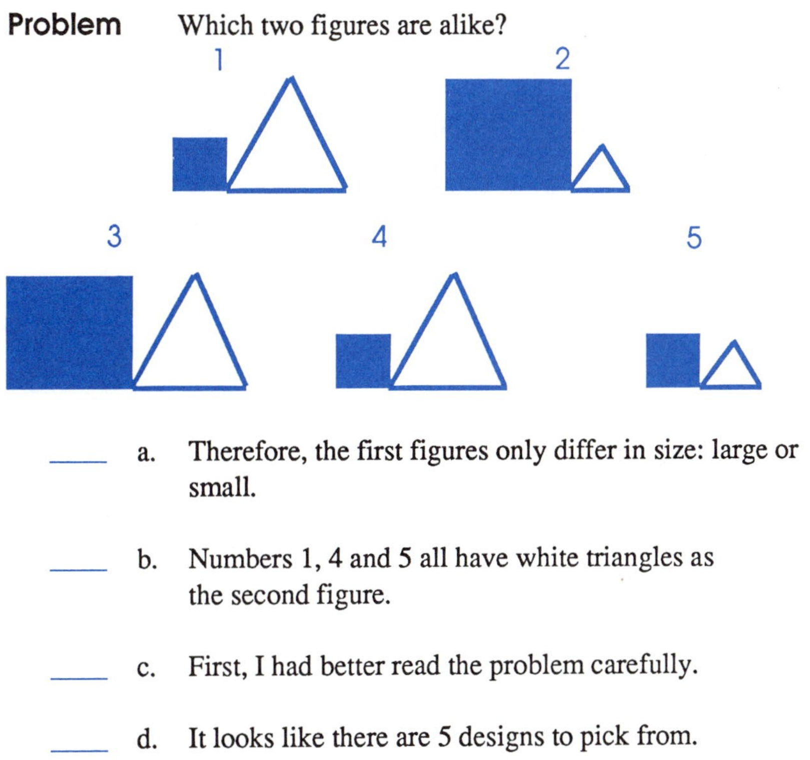

____ a. Therefore, the first figures only differ in size: large or small.

____ b. Numbers 1, 4 and 5 all have white triangles as the second figure.

____ c. First, I had better read the problem carefully.

____ d. It looks like there are 5 designs to pick from.

____ e. Numbers 2 and 3 both have large first figures; does that mean they are exactly the same?

____ f. Yes, the right answer must be figures 1 and 4.

____ g. All five designs have two figures in each of them.

____ h. I guess I'll start by comparing each design's first figure.

____ i. Nope, numbers 2 and 3 aren't the same; their second figures are both white triangles, but they are different sizes.

____ j. Numbers 1, 4 and 5 have second figures that are different in size: 1 is large, 4 is large, and 5 is small.

____ k. I wonder how many designs I have to choose from?

____ l. So next I guess I need to compare the three designs that all have small first figures: 1, 4 and 5.

____ m. First, I'll look at those designs that have large first figures.

____ n. All of the designs have two colors: black and white.

____ o. I'd better check my answer: both 1 and 4 have small black rectangles first, then large white triangles second.

____ p. Therefore it cannot be number 5, so the answer should be numbers 1 and 4.

____ q. All of the first figures are rectangles and are black.

____ r. Therefore the answer cannot be 2 and 3, so I'll cross them out.

____ s. Now that I know what kinds of designs I have to choose from, where do I start?

____ t. How do the second figures compare in designs 1, 4 and 5?

____ u. Now, let's see, what are the five designs?

This problem perhaps seems very complicated. It is easier if you remember to use some mental skills taught earlier in this book. In particular, think about grouping of information. Would it be helpful to divide those steps into logical groups and then try to sequence each group separately? Draw on all that you have learned in mastering this exercise. Use this space for grouping if it helps.

Share your answers with others in your class. Compare them and debate any differences. Change your sequence if you wish, based on the discussion.

Think About It!

If you had to purchase Thinking Tools for $25 each, which ones would you purchase in order to solve this problem?

Chapter Eleven

Thinking: The Ability And The Will

Thinking for a living — and for a lifetime — ultimately depends on whether or not we are willing.

This book should have helped you recognize the role that clear, conscious thinking plays in almost every aspect of our lives — our jobs, our schooling, our relations with other people. Thinking is one of our most constant and important human activities, whether we are aware of it or not. We cannot help thinking and choosing. Our fundamental choice is not whether or not to think but rather to think well or to think poorly.

Hopefully this book has also helped you recognize that you have the mental skills needed for thinking well. A final question for you to consider, though, is this one: What keeps you from thinking well, given that you have the ability? What forces in yourself and in the world around you interfere with your ability or willingness to think clearly, fully, and honestly? Here are some of those pitfalls to clear thinking. As you read them, try to identify cases when each of them has hampered your own thinking.

Emotions

Sometimes we think poorly when we are nervous, angry, excited, frustrated, frightened or under pressure. Often our desires get in the way of clear thinking. Acknowledging our emotions is a valid, important part of the thinking process. Unfortunately those same emotions can also interfere with that process.

Habits

Often we do not even notice that we have a choice because we make it so habitually. Habitual thinking is useful unless it becomes a substitute for clear thinking.

Functional Fixedness

Functional fixedness is our tendency to see only one point of view, rather than several alternatives. Examples would be: "Math is for the classroom, not for calculating best bargains in the store;" "A woman's place is in the home or in a secretarial position;" or "This course is over, so I'll never need to open that book again." Functional fixedness leads us to ignore other possibilities, other uses or other solutions beyond the very obvious.

Self-Confidence

Our belief in ourselves dramatically affects our thinking. If we are **externally controlled**, we look to others, to fate, or somewhere else for our decisions; we feel no control over our lives. We have no faith in our own abilities and see little need to think through our own decisions. If we are **internally controlled** and have a sense of our own capability, we may more often think things through since the choice is ours alone. We have more confidence in our ability to make choices. Both confidence and orientation affect clear thinking.

Laziness

Thinking is often hard work. Many of us are tempted to do the easiest thing or to let someone else think it through, because active thinking seems to be too much trouble.

Not Knowing Where To Start

The situation facing us sometimes seems so confusing, unfamiliar, or threatening that we don't know where to begin. We can "freeze" and go blank. We can become immediately frustrated and give up. We can do the wrong thing.

Time

Often we must think choices through in a few seconds or minutes. We can use our Thinking Tools in that short span of time, but it still hampers us in many ways, such as by limiting the amount of information we can get and use.

Information Flaws

Sometimes we have too little information. Sometimes we have the wrong information. Often our thinking is hampered by uncertainty over what relevant information we do or do not have. All of us have observed others making decisions while unaware they are missing some vital information. Knowing what we do not know is a key to using information for thinking.

Apparent Lack Of Mental Tools

Even when we seem to know what needs to be done in thinking a problem through, we can feel crippled by not knowing how to go about it.

Others' Opinions

Our thinking is often affected by others. They may have opinions about what we should do. We may fear their judgements on what we decide. We may consider conforming to their ways more important than thinking something through ourselves.

These factors hamper all of us in our thinking. Some of them interfere mainly with our ability to think clearly. Most of them, however, interfere more with our willingness to think clearly. Conscious, effective thinking depends on both of these factors: the ability and the will. We must be able to think clearly, and we must want to think clearly.

The discoveries about your thinking that you have made in this book should help you with those pitfalls dealing with your ability to think clearly. Your Thinking Toolkit, for example, should prepare you to avoid the pitfall of not knowing where to start with a choice. You now know how to start wrestling with a problem; you are aware of many mental tools you can use.

How about those pitfalls relating to willingness to think clearly? That is an individual matter, and one which awaits you beyond this book. Are you confident of your ability to think clearly? Are you likely to put forth the effort to think things through instead of deciding by habit? Are you willing to break out of functional fixedness and to see alternatives to a situation?

Those are questions which can only be answered by each person individually. Moreover, like the Thinking Tools themselves, these issues of willingness to think are also changeable parts of your personality. If you keep practicing testing hypotheses, you will become better at it and more prepared to use it as a mental tool. Similarly, if you keep practicing self-confidence — your belief in yourself as an effective thinker who is in charge of your own destiny — you will find yourself strong and capable in that area.

This book, then, is a beginning rather than an end. It has tried to help you discover a set of mental tools and ways of using them. It has tried to show you that you have the ability. Discovering and practicing the will to think clearly is a journey of self-discovery which you must take on your own.

Think About It!

VERMONT STATE COLLEGES
0 0003 0423635 9